ADVANCE PRAISE FOR THE EVOLUTIONARY LEADER

"Anyone interested in taking her/ his performance to another level will treasure The Evolutionary Leader. It describes simple, yet powerful, principles that deliver dramatic results. I love the principles of "do less and achieve more" and "presence equals performance" but find it actually difficult to highlight these 2 since I consider the whole book as an extraordinary asset for my personal development."

Thomas Träger – Country President at Schneider Electric Denmark

"A new model for leadership success. Timothy J. Carroll's The Evolutionary Leader will not only lift your performance but shift your understanding of yourself and others as human beings."

Ali Brown – Entrepreneur, Mentor, Angel Investor

"A powerful, easy-to-read, and hugely inspiring book. If you are willing to truly understand how you work as a person, The Evolutionary Leader will help you dramatically improve your leadership skills."

Peter Johansson – CEO at Image Systems AB

"Timothy J. Carroll, with the agility of the athlete he is, leads us through the rules and regimens of evolutionary leadership with precision and skill, to help you dramatically improve performance—yours and others'."

Alan Weiss, PhD - Author of *Million Dollar Consulting, Million Dollar Maverick*, and over 60 other books

"Timothy J. Carroll dissects the way our mind works when we're performing, whether that's on a sports field or in a boardroom. Having laid bare the mechanisms of the conscious and subconscious minds, he then shows you how to 'be super present' and take the way you operate to the next level."

William Trubridge – World Champion and Double World Record Holding Freediver

"The Evolutionary Leader will give you the power to completely change your life and help you achieve your dreams, goals, and superior performance. This book should be read over and over again and become a lighthouse in your life, supporting you on how to navigate in this new world. Be who you always wanted to be, enjoy the journey, and start now the evolution in you."

David Nicholl – Country Director, Rockwell Automation - UK & Ireland

THE

EVOLUTIONARY

LEADER

5 steps to dramatically develop

people and performance

TIMOTHY J. CARROLL

THE EVOLUTIONARY LEADER

5 steps to dramatically develop people and performance

DEDICATION

We all stand on the shoulders of giants who have come before us. This book is for all of those people who have had an impact and influence on me and on my journey. Thank you for helping to shape my life.

ACKNOWLEDGEMENTS

THANK YOU TO Alicia Dunams, my book coach, and all of her support staff who have made this book possible. To Matt Wallden, my health consultant, whom I started this process with and interviewed. To my beloved wife for believing in me and supporting me through the process of the creation of this book – I'm immensely grateful. I would also like to thank my team, Jimmy, Jake, and Mabelle, who tirelessly worked behind the scenes under great pressure to hit rigorous deadlines.

To the people in my life who have lifted me up and inspired me: Dr. Alan Weiss, thank you for showing me how valuable I am. Dr. Stephen Covey, thank you for your seven habits and the legacy you have left. Dr. Deepak Chopra, for reminding me who I am. Sandford Perrett, for showing me who I am. Eckhart Tolle, for keeping me on track. Pablo Friedlander, thank you for helping me to dive deep. Tony Robbins, your example showed me the way. Dr. Tad James, Dr. Michael Hall, Michelle Duval and Jeanette

Mantel, thank you for teaching me the skills to help so many people.

Special thanks to those people who have trusted me over the years to support them in attaining their goals and allowed me to facilitate their development. I am humbled, honoured, and forever grateful. To those who have come into my life when I needed it the most and changed its trajectory, thank you for believing in me, teaching me the skills, giving me the insight, and opening doors when they were closed.

To my heroes, Michael Jackson, Michael Jordan, Mohammed Ali, Nelson Mandela, Gandhi, and Martin Luther King, thank you for standing tall and being brave.

To all my friends, coaches, and competitors around the world and in New Zealand who pushed me and helped shape me as an athlete. There are too many to name in full, but I would like to make special mention of Rob and Fred Groen, Damon Rundstrom, Michael Cordell, Shelley May, Glen and Alan, John Pennay, Adam Keramea, Richard Silver, Ron Scarpa, and Brett Wing.

To my parents, who gave me the best start possible; thank you for your love and support and providing the launching platform from which I could fly. To my brother, I miss you. To my ancestors who came before me, thank you for helping me to be a good ancestor and leave the world a better place than I found it. Finally, to my children and their children, may this serve as an offering to your evolution and to the evolution of the human race.

THE EVOLUTIONARY LEADER

INTRODUCTION

HAVING BEEN INVOLVED in a myriad of sports at a young age, I decided to commit to barefoot water-skiing when I was 16 after injuring my knee while playing rugby. My father was one of the founding members of the New Zealand Barefoot Water-ski Club in the early 70's. I learnt to water-ski when I was 10 and barefoot water-ski at the age of 12. Over the period of a 16-year career, I went on to represent New Zealand and compete in 4 world championships. Sport was my focus, and I was committed to improving my performance and being the best skier I could possibly be.

After turning 21, I came to a roadblock on my journey. It seemed that it didn't matter how much physical or technical training I did, I just wasn't improving. So I looked into the mental side of sport and sports psychology. I was introduced to a local sports psychologist in Wellington, and we started to do some work together. Learning new techniques and having breakthroughs, as well as someone to talk with, started to pay dividends. My performance began to improve, and I started breaking personal bests in competitions. I was on to something, and it dawned on me that the mental game of sport was just as important, if not more so, than the physical game.

This turning point started me on a path that has led to a career which has spanned the last 20 years and encompassed learning from some of the best performance coaches/experts in the world, then starting my own business and working with world-class athletes and leaders, helping them perform to their potential. Having worked with hundreds of clients, I have consistently seen that results come and performance improves when people learn about, embrace, and begin to work with their mental/emotional game, as well as their physical and technical one. This is working with the whole person. Sport, like business, is a game that is played in the mind as much as with the body. It is to this endeavour that I share what I have learned through trial and error, as well as from the world's best to support you, the reader, to be all you can be and leave your legacy in the world, making it a better place.

Leaders are readers, and it is no coincidence that the words are so similar. Read comes from Old English *rǣdan*, of Germanic origin; related to Dutch **raden** and German *raten 'advise, guess.'* Early senses included 'advise' and 'interpret (a riddle or dream'). Rede, a verb which is a variant of read, means the advice or counsel given by one person to another. *What is your rede?*

Leadership is a topic that is dear to my heart. I wrote this book for the current and future leaders of the world because there is a clear pattern that I see when leaders come to me for my support. They are often deficient in the knowledge of how people really work. They want to learn how to get the best out of themselves and their people, supporting them to perform to their best. Of course, this cannot happen if they have not learned to do this for themselves first, which is the challenge. Therefore, when working with Presidents, CEO's, and Directors of multi-national firms, we always start with themselves first, helping them to be the change they want to see in the world and a role model of what is possible to others.

There is a paradigm shift happening in the world at the moment. It is an evolution of consciousness and, ultimately, behaviour. There are two worlds in leadership, two forces that are opposing, as well as pulling against, one another. One is the "Transactional Leader," and the other is the "Transformational Leader," both of which are very different styles of leadership. Transaction means an instance of buying or selling something; the action of conducting business; an exchange or interaction between people. As a word, it is derived from late Latin **transactio(n-)**, from **transigere 'drive through.'** And so this is the style of the transactional leader, the action of conducting business, through commercial transactions, driving the results through exchanges or interactions between people—driving the results being the thrust of the style. This type of leadership has a time and a place, but when it is done all of the time and is the *Modeus Operandi* of the leader, it is destructive and affects the culture of the organization negatively. Over time this results in demotivating the people and causing low engagement in the staff and ultimately poor performance and results for the organization.

On the other hand, to "transform" means to make a marked change in the form, nature, or appearance of, or to undergo a marked change. The prefix "trans" means across; beyond; or to the other side of. Into another state or place: *transform | translate.* Surpassing; transcending. Therefore, transformational leadership is to make a marked change, move beyond to the other side, surpassing or transcending the current form. Transformational leaders are interested in doing this throughout the business, mostly through the people themselves. Transformational leaders lead companies through the transformation of the people, culture, and its leadership. The result is the positive transformation of the business resulting in positive growth and a high-performing culture that is engaged and self-motivated.

The current paradigm falls with the transactional leader; this is the dominant force in the world of leadership. These forces create a lot of tension, and it is this tension that creates change. Change is coming to leadership, and we will see what the outcome will be from this tug of war. What is clear in my work is that there are many leaders starting to wake up to the realization that there is a better way to lead, a way that gets better results and achieves them more easily and effortlessly. This is the way of the transformational leader, and they want to learn how to be this type of leader. They are good managers, good transactional leaders, and they know how to do this well, but when it comes to transformational leadership and taking a company to the next level through its people, they are not equipped. My hope is that the coming chapters will lend a hand to the understandings of how people work to give leaders some tools to bridge this divide.

The science of behavioural change and human potential is vast. To really understand the different things that are driving you, how you're hard-wired and created, is vital for success. Some people are born with all the right programming and the right gifts and don't need to work on themselves or learn things, because they're naturally in them, but that's a very rare person. Most people who have succeeded in life have gone forward and worked on themselves, learned from others, and then applied that in their life.

Developing performance is an art and a science that is not taught to us in school. We are not taught the secrets of top performance or how we work as human beings. Sharing the knowledge I have learned along my journey which has contributed to supporting my clients and own self to break through to higher performance is part of my purpose. I would be remiss if I took this knowledge with me to my grave, and so it is with great pleasure I share with you five of the top lessons for high performance that can be applied to any context or chosen field to break through to the next level. If embraced and utilized consistently, they will revolutionize how you think and perform on a consistent basis. Achieving this is up to you.

No one can make you change; you have to want it and want it bad. Are you ready to take things to the next level? Will you commit to applying the knowledge in the following chapters to see how it works? Are you ready to be all you want to be and even help others do the same? As Abraham Maslow, the Einstein of Psychology, pointed to his students and asked, "Which one of you wants to be the next iconic musician, business leader, politician, or athlete? Is it you? Or will it be you?" After a long silence, he would say … "Well, if not you, then who?" Maslow challenged his students to be all they could be, and this is the challenge I put to you. The next moment is not guaranteed, and time is of the essence. We are not getting out of this one alive. My wish is that the following chapters support you to make your mark in the world and leave it a little bit better than you found it for the ones who inherit it from us.

Who do you want to become? What legacy do you want to leave? How do you want to be remembered when your time is up?

Are you with me? Let's make it so.

Timothy J. Carroll

"Be the change that you wish to see in the world!"

~ **Mahatma Gandhi**

1.

MASTERY OF YOUR MIND

"Simple can be harder than complex: You have to work hard to get your thinking clean to make it simple. But it's worth it in the end because once you get there, you can move mountains."

~ **Steve Jobs**

STUDIES SHOW THAT scientists have not been able to find the mind. The mind is discussed, somewhat understood, and even defined in the Apple dictionary, but not located, so to speak, in the physical body. Does it exist if it can't be found physically? The mystery of the mind brings up some essential questions … What is the mind? Why do we have one? How does it work? How do we use it to our advantage?

The mind runs the body, and all of sport, all of business, is made up of behaviours. If we're not in charge of our mind, we're not in charge of our behaviours. Therefore, behaving correctly in the context that we're in means that we're getting great performance. To understand the mind supports the understanding of how you work as a human being. It's not something we learned as we grew up as children, so we don't really understand how we work as human beings. Whether we're leaders running a top business, athletes trying to achieve our goals, or Mums and Dads leading a family, we're really trying to perform to our best, but without a manual to show us how to get the best out of ourselves. Therefore, to understand how we work as human beings is to empower ourselves and support us in getting the best out of ourselves day in and day out.

A large percentage of the population on the planet is actually under the control of their own mind. Their mind is driving the bus. One of the biggest things we can do in life is to learn how to get in charge of our own selves, to lead ourselves to understand how to create change within ourselves and get back in that driving seat, taking control of the bus. That's what this book is going to help you do.

How many of us learned about the human mind in high school? How many have contemplated the above questions, discussed them around the class, and learned about them from our teachers? The nature of the mind and how it works is not considered important to learn about. Yet it is the most powerful instrument known to man, and it exists within every one of us, every day, determining our perception, what we experience, and creating our results. Let's start to look at our own nature, answer some

The most powerful computer known to human kind does not exist out there somewhere in the world; it exists within us.

of the above questions, and unravel the mystery of our mind.

The human mind operates like a computer. In fact, there are two distinctive minds within every one of us that psychology has known about for decades. We have the conscious mind, or the thinking mind, and the unconscious mind, or the doing mind. The conscious mind is the one that judges and critics the world and the results we are getting. Then there is the unconscious mind, the one that is doing everything for us without us having to think about it. For example, hitting the golf ball out of the bunker or hitting the tennis ball down the line to win the point, walking down the street, or responding to a situation in the office.

We have built computers in the image of our own selves. The problem is that the average person knows more about their MacBook or PC than they do about how their own computer works. Let's have a look at this computer within so we can start to get a grip on how it works and how to use it to create the results we want in our life.

Diagram of the Conscious Mind and Unconscious Mind

Our Two Selves

Conscious Mind

(Thinking Mind)

Subconscious Mind

(Doing Mind)

By Dr. Tad James, Advanced Neuro Dynamics © 1995

There are many different ways to support people to change, get different results, and improve their performance. There are many practical tools to use, and I will share some of these with you later on in the book. To do this and do it well, it is important to understand the psychology of human beings and how to create change within a person neurologically. People can change, and people do change quickly all of the time.

My hope is that by reading this book you will learn something about the psychology of how you work and take away some practical tools that will support you in being all you can be. People can learn to work with themselves from the inside out and support themselves in changing their behaviours, creating new habits.

That's the key to performing to your potential and creating what you want in your life—to work with yourself consciously, with your unconscious mind and the software within it. To actually remove the programming that sabotages you from being all you can be and reprogramming yourself for success. To perform at your best, you must align your inner game with the results you want to get in your outer game. There are many techniques and ways to do this, which we will cover in this and the coming chapters.

Our Internal Computer

The Unconscious Mind

The unconscious mind or subconscious mind is described in the MacBook dictionary as:

Subconscious – the part of one's mind which one is not fully aware of but influences one's actions and feelings. Not used in psychoanalysis where they prefer to use the word

When we change ourselves, we change our results

Unconscious mind.

Unconscious mind – the part of the mind, which the conscious mind, does not have access to and which affects behaviours and emotions.

As you can see, they are the same things and have the same function. This part of us is actually super conscious, as it acts like the hard drive in our computer, in charge of all the memory, programming, and output. These actions are all happening outside of our conscious awareness. The bottom line is *the unconscious mind is in charge of all learning, behaviour, and change*. Whether we like it or not, these things are happening all of the time; and if we want to improve our ability to do the above, we must learn about how the unconscious mind works, or all of our learning, behaviour, and change will be unconscious and happen to us outside of our awareness.

> The unconscious mind is in charge of all learning, behaviour, and change

Prime Directives of the Unconscious Mind

1. Stores all of your memories.
2. Organizes all of your memories, in a linear fashion.
3. It's the place where your emotions come from and

are stored.

4. Represses memories with unresolved negative emotions.

5. It represses memories to protect you.

6. Brings these repressed memories up for "resolution."

7. Runs the body; e.g. beats your heart, etc.

8. Preserves the body; e.g. fight or flight instinct.

9. It's a servant that follows orders from the conscious mind.

10. It controls and maintains all of your perceptions or your experiences.

11. It's in charge of making, storing, and transmitting energy in the body.

12. It maintains instincts, creates habits, and learns through repetition.

13. It works on the premise that things are either right or wrong; it is moralistic.

14. It is programmed to seek more and more.

15. It takes everything personally.

16. Works on the principle of Least Effort: Do less and achieve more.

17. Does not process negatives.

18. Functions best as a whole integrated unit.

Tad James, Advanced Neuro Dynamics 1995

The Software

Within our hard drive, or unconscious, we have software running, just like in our computer. These are programs that the unconscious uses to create our perception, experience, and behaviours, or in other words, the outputs. A computer does not work unless information is put into it, and then it creates an output. The same goes for us. Information is coming in through our five senses, and we then filter this information unconsciously through our unconscious mind, and on the screen of our mind, we get an experience. This experience is made up of pictures we see, sounds we hear, feelings we feel, both internally and externally, smells, tastes, and our internal dialogue or self-talk.

It is the programs within the unconscious that determine what our experience is and, therefore, our perception of things. *This then determines our behaviour and the results that we get.*

When working with clients, I am most interested, not in the presenting problems they share with me, but in what is going on within their programs which is creating the problem, performance, or result they are experiencing. Only then can we find out what the root cause is, and only then can we do something about it, creating a behavioural change and new result.

Some of the software within the unconscious mind that determines our experiences are:

1. **Beliefs**, what we believe is what we achieve. A belief is a thought that has been reinforced by another or ourselves and said "yes" to until we believe it to be true or real. Some beliefs serve us— for example, "The world is a safe place." Some beliefs don't serve us, such as, "Money is hard to make." These are called limiting or negative beliefs.

2. **Values**, are what is important to us in the different contexts of life—for example, career, health, relationships, etc. What is important to us is where we spend our time, and where we spend our time determines how we behave. Values affect our behaviour, depending on the context, and they also influence our motivation. If what is important to us in our career is being fulfilled, then we will be highly motivated and engaged.

3. **Thinking Preferences** are our preferred ways of thinking in different contexts. They are also called meta-programs and are our perceptual filters, kind of like sunglasses that we put on that help us see the world in a new light. For example, is the glass half

full or is it half empty; are you motivated by a carrot or by a stick; do you agree with people or prefer to disagree? These are just three of over 60+ known programs that determine our perception.

The Best Relationship Between our Two Selves

It was actually Tim Gallwey, the author of *The Inner Game of Tennis,* in 1974 who discovered how the two selves best relate with each other. He was observing tennis players in a game, and he noticed that they started talking to themselves, mostly critiquing themselves and beating themselves up mentally on the tennis court. For example, "Oh, that was a bad shot," or, "Oh, come on, you can do better than that!" His observations led him to wonder, *who are they talking to?*

He understood that there are two selves within each of us, the conscious self and the unconscious self, and they relate with each other all the time. Through his observations and coaching, he discovered the best relationship to have between these two selves is one of a loving parent to a child. What Timothy is telling us is the key to better performance lies in building a positive working relationship between the instructing conscious mind and the doing unconscious mind.

"The development of inner skills is required, but it is interesting to note that if, while learning tennis, you begin to learn how to focus your attention and how to trust in yourself, you have learned something far more valuable than how to hit a forceful backhand."

~ Timothy Gallwey

So, how do we do that?

Dr. Tad James explains there are three things we can focus on that will support us in having the best relationship possible with ourselves and others to support top performance.

Trust. We trust others and ourselves. Remember, the unconscious is the doing mind. If we are playing a game of golf and need to hit the ball out of a bunker, the best way to achieve this, if we have done the training and know how to play the shot, is to *trust* that we can do it.

Non-judgmental. When we are non-judgemental toward others and ourselves, we accept

We are non-judgmental to others, and ourselves, which means that we accept everything as it is and are not critical toward ourselves in any way.

32

everything as it is allowing us to stay present. When playing a game of golf, if we talk to ourselves negatively, telling ourselves how badly we played that last hole or shot, this is an example of being judgmental of one's self.

Positively Encouraging. We positively encourage others and ourselves. Being positive and telling ourselves, "You can do it," or asking great questions like, "What's the opportunity here?" allows us to feel good and optimistic. When playing a game of golf, tell yourself before the putt that it's going in, see it in your mind's eye, and remind yourself that you can do it.

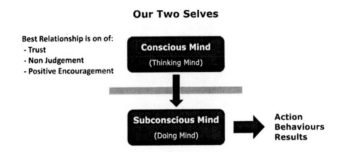

Diagram of Conscious Mind communicating with Unconscious Mind.

How to Improve Your Relationship with Yourself and Others to Develop Performance

1. Be aware of the two selves, and remember that you are communicating with both your own and others' unconscious doing mind all of the time.

2. There are no good or bad performances; it's all feedback.

3. Trust, practice acceptance, and encourage yourself and others until it becomes a habit.

4. Provide the unconscious mind with visual instructions to support it in achieving what you want to achieve. See it the way you want it to happen.

5. Ask yourself great questions. "What is the opportunity in this situation?" The question will drive the answer and focus. The better the question, the better the result.

Practice the five steps above, and you will see that performance will improve and be more consistent in your chosen endeavour. Those people who do relate that way with themselves and with others will get the best out of themselves and the best out of other people.

I was working with a golfer in Sweden on his mental game. He had a habit of being very critical of himself while playing. If he played a "bad shot," he would really punish and berate himself. So we discussed the results of that and if it was helping him play better golf—and he agreed that it wasn't. So we had a look at a different way that he could relate with and communicate with himself. I taught him the five steps above, and he put them into practice. When he hit a so-called bad shot, instead of berating himself, he would look at the opportunity in his next shot and how he could perform to his best. He would encourage himself and say, "Come on, you can do it. You have done this a million times," and his self-talk was much better, compared to beating himself up or talking negatively to himself. This player ended up taking a number of shots off his handicap and performing much better, just from that simple intervention.

Self-Talk

The thinking mind, or conscious mind, is in charge of the self-talk or internal dialogue that goes on inside. Being conscious of this and paying attention to what we say to others and ourselves is critical in getting the best out of our unconscious doing mind, which is in charge of all our behaviour. What we say to ourselves is being listened to by every cell in our body. Dr. Deepak Chopra, one of the world's foremost experts on the mind/body connection, tells us that every cell in our body listens to every thought in our mind. This is a good example of our subconscious mind listening to everything that our conscious mind says. We have to be aware of what we're saying to ourselves. Those people who have succeeded in life, perform to their full potential, or achieved their potential in life are the ones who have great self-talk, talking with themselves very positively.

One prime example of this is Muhammad Ali, renowned as the greatest athlete of all time. When he was in his late teens, he started to tell himself that he was the greatest: "I am the greatest." He kept telling himself that and praising himself, and programming his unconscious mind to believe what was necessary to become the greatest. When interviewed later in his life about why he kept saying he was the greatest, he said, "Well, if I tell myself enough, then it's just a matter of time before I believe it." What we believe is what we achieve, and in this example, Ali is describing one way to program the unconscious mind for success.

How to Improve Your Self-talk for Top Performance

For top performance, you have to become 100% conscious of what you're talking to yourself about and stop talking negatively to yourself. Replace that with positive self-talk. Write down what it is that you want to achieve. Write it as if you already have it; e.g. I am leading a team that leads themselves, we have achieved _____ and are celebrating that together at our end-of-year party.

Program this into your unconscious by seeing it in your mind's eye. Visualize the end result, the accomplishment of what you have achieved. Do this in the morning when you wake up and in the evening before you go to sleep for two minutes each time.

During the day, if you hear yourself talking about yourself in a negative way, catch yourself and stop it. Then affirm the opposite until you get a strong positive feeling inside. Stay true to this thought, put your attention on it, write it down and focus on it, repeat it to yourself until you 100% believe it. Then you will achieve it!

Why Change?

It's your choice. You can stay unconscious and be struggling away, have negative belief systems or programs running – wondering why you're not able to achieve what you want, when another person in the same family or company is striving ahead and doing very well, achieving their goals and creating what they want. Or you can take responsibility to change and learn what it takes to do that, apply that, and upgrade your own programming.

You can work with your hard drive or your unconscious mind and actually program yourself for success—and that's your potential right there. You

What we believe is what we achieve.

have the ability to program yourself for success – do you

know how? You are about to learn some of the techniques that will support you in creating a paradigm shift in performance for yourself and others.

The Inner Game

"Everything is created twice.
First on the inside, then on the outside."
~ Stephen Covey

The inner game, a term coined by Timothy Gallwey, is the sum total of our programming that has been created over the period of our lifetime. In fact, most of our core programming is created before the age of 10 years old. Your thoughts and the feelings originate from this programming. If you have a lot of negative belief systems, you'll have a lot of negative focus and negative thinking arising in different contexts. It's your programming that determines your thinking, feelings, communication, and behaviour. Positive programming creates positive thinking and positive feelings. Therefore, it's our inner game that determines the results in our outer game of life, business, health, or sport.

If nothing changes— nothing changes!

We are programmed in different contexts—whether it is in our career, relationships, or in health. We have different belief systems, different programs, and values; and they're determining our results in those contexts, whether we like it or not. If you don't like your results, then you'd better have a look at your programming and make some changes. Dr. Michael Hall calls this 'the matrix' of your mind. In the iconic movie *The Matrix*, the people who were plugged into it experienced a projected reality in their minds made by the machines. Just like this, you're experiencing your reality on the movie screen of your mind in every waking moment. The picture you see is light hitting the cones and rods at the back of your eye and sending a signal to your brain. The matrix or programming in your neurology creates your experience.

The projector is your mind, the movie reel your programming, and your experience is the movie screen. If you want to change the movie, you have got to change the reel or your programming. This is your responsibility, no one else's. Are you ready to change now?

Ignorance is Bliss

Henrik Stenson from Sweden is one of the world's best golf players. He has a mental coach, Torsten Hansson. Together they are one of the greatest teams in the golfing world. I was asked to work for the Swedish Golf Federation as a mental skills coach supporting the Swedish amateur players along with other coaches around Sweden. Torsten headed up the network of mental coaches around Sweden. While at a conference in Stockholm, he mentioned something that he focuses on with Henrik that makes a big difference to his performance. The premise is, make everything that is unknown known so that there are no surprises. Have good intel, scout out the environment, and make sure you are familiar with the territory of where you will be playing and staying.

In cognitive behavioural sciences, we have a similar premise. *Make all that is unconscious conscious to create better results.* If you're in the business of performing to your best or if you're unsatisfied with your results, you've got to start to look within at some of the programming that you've got going on inside and make a change. *You don't know what you don't know.* To make what is unknown known is my definition of what taking responsibility for your results means. Your programing is in your unconscious mind; you are not aware of it, yet it determines the results that you

> **The premise is, make everything that is unknown known so that there are no surprises.**

get in your life. To change, you have to become conscious of it to do something about it. Are you ready?

In the early 2000's, I worked with a client who could not get pregnant. When she first came to me, she was very stressed about it. In fact, she'd been twice to have IVF, and it hadn't worked; they'd been trying for two or three years. So we had a look at her emotions around her issue and what her belief systems were, and we found a significant amount of negative beliefs around getting pregnant. She actually didn't believe that it was possible, and there was a lot of stress and negative emotions caught up inside around the whole process. It is very stressful to really want a baby and not be able to become pregnant. Using specific techniques from cognitive behavioural sciences to release the negative emotions and beliefs, replacing them with positive beliefs, we made the changes inside; it took just a few sessions.

After we completed the intervention and tested the new programming and how she felt, she was calm and at peace with her past. She was able to accept things as they were. She believed sincerely that she would get pregnant and that it was just a matter of time. She left, deciding not to continue with IVF but to try naturally with her husband without any attachment to a result. A few months later, I got a phone call from her saying that she was pregnant, and she was so happy, thanking me very much for my support and work. It was so rewarding to make a difference to her and her family. When she let go and started to focus on the positive and the opportunities and what a beautiful future she would have when she was pregnant, it really prepared her body – remember, every cell in the body listens to every thought we have, consciously and unconsciously.

Another case of how easy it is to change was a lady who had a phobia of flying. She felt it was so limiting because she could not go on holiday in Europe with her grown children. She came to me because she wanted to let go of her fear of flying in order to improve the quality of her life and to have choices. In just two one-hour sessions, we worked together to let go of the deep fear from her unconscious, as well as a specific trauma she'd had while flying when she was much younger. After testing her newfound perception of flying and making sure she was 100% convinced that she could fly again, she mustered up the courage to book a flight to Spain. I got a thank you card in the mail from Spain, saying how happy she was to fly again. These are some great examples of people who have decided that enough is enough, I need to change; and they sought out the right person to support them in that, made the change, and created different results. So can you!

When I was in my early 20s, competing for New Zealand in barefoot water-skiing, we attended the World Championships in Florida. The weekend before the World Championships, we had a practice tournament. I was very well prepared, the water conditions were perfect, and I was psyched to get on the water and put everything into practice. In the tricks event, I made a perfect first pass and threw the rope away at the end of the run. As I was sinking into the water, a thought popped into my head, *that was so good, I bet you fall off next run.* I was lying there in the water, struggling with this thought and wanting it to go away, but the more I struggled with it, the more it persisted. The boat came back to me, and I gave them my instructions. I started my second pass, and on a very basic trick, I fell, BAM! and found myself lying in the water.

In that moment, I had a breakthrough. I realized that my thoughts create my results. That the negative thought that I could not get rid of out of head had led

> I realized that my thoughts create my results.

to me falling off in an uncharacteristic manner. Not everyone is lucky enough to have that breakthrough regarding the power of our attention—that what we focus on is what we create; that every thought is listened to by every cell of the body; that our thoughts, conscious and unconscious, control our behaviour and results.

As Henry Ford said, *"If we believe we'll get it or if we believe we won't—both are right."* I had a paradigm shift in my thinking while lying there in the water that day, and that was the beginning of my journey, leading me to write this book.

Three Things to Stop Doing for Top Performance

The Blame Game

Stop blaming others and making excuses for your results. People stuck in the blame game are unable to take responsibility for their results. They are totally at the effect of everything outside of themselves. People who blame are not able to respond creatively to situations, circumstances, and people; they just react. This means they are a victim of their past conditioning and they project it onto the now. A stimulus occurs, and then they get triggered and react according to their conditioning. There is no choice, no freedom, and no power in being stuck in this game. People tend to stay stuck and disempowered, continuing to create, yes, create the same results. Eventually, after experiencing enough pain and suffering, some decide that this game does not work anymore, and they try something else. This is one of the top things that stop people from taking responsibility and looking within. They believe that the problem is out there and not in themselves.

As the mouse Zed explains in the Deepak Malhotra's book, *I moved your cheese*, *"... the problem is not that the mouse is in the maze, but the maze is in the mouse."*

You Become Who You Associate With

The next thing to avoid that stops you from achieving top performance is hanging out with people who may hold you back or who are stuck in their lives. I learned many years ago that *if you want to be the best, go and hang out with the best*. Whatever you want to succeed in, find people who have succeeded in that already and be open and humble enough to actually learn from them. With an open mind and curious attitude, you will learn more from them than you can possibly imagine and perhaps then will make it your own and even take it to the next level.

> If you want to fly like an eagle, don't hang around with turkeys.

Ignore Negative Inner Dialogue

Last, and probably most important, is to stop believing all that stuff that's going on inside your mind. Actually pay attention and listen to all of your thoughts and stop believing what your mind is saying to you. I challenge you to one day just take a voice recorder and, without any form of censoring, speak whatever comes into your mind. Don't stop—just talk and keep talking into the microphone uncensored until you can't speak anymore. You will be amazed at all the rubbish that comes spewing out of your mind when you listen back to it. The best thing is what comes next; take the time to speak your truth into the recorder after you've listened back to your mind dump. The mind becomes quiet, clear, and you have access to your inner wisdom, which comes forth when all those thoughts stop now.

William Trubridge, a friend of mine from New Zealand, now living not far from me in the Bahamas on Long Island, is the World Record Holder in the Constant Weight No Fins (CNF) discipline. This is the most pure form of Free Diving, where with just a breath and his goggles, William has dived down to 101m or 331 feet and come back to the surface. One day, we were having lunch together, and I interviewed him regarding his experience when he dives.

I asked him, "What are you thinking about when diving deep into the ocean?" He told me that thoughts come up in his mind, like *this is the last breath you will ever take* or *turn back, you are going to die.*

Still your mind and come to your senses.

He went on to say that he's so bored with all that negative thinking that goes on inside, he doesn't pay attention to it anymore. He ignores it, and, therefore, it doesn't have control over him. I asked him, "What are you paying attention to?" and he said, "I'm paying attention to the silence between my thoughts, and the more I pay attention to that, the deeper I dive into that silence, the deeper I can dive into the ocean."

This is a metaphor for life. William and others who perform to their best, break world records, or are respected as leaders have found that when they are able to still their mind and come to their senses, they are able to get out of the way of themselves and perform to their best. Later in this book, we are going to explore this in depth and look into why this is and how to do it.

How to Create Change

How can you proactively work with the most powerful computer in the world, your own self, to create top performance and achieve the results you want? The way to do this is to work with your programs, the filters that determine your experience. What sort of movie is being projected onto the screen of your mind? As a consultant and coach, the most effective way to create change is to work with the person's inner game and help them reprogram their software to create the results they want. If you are not getting what you want, you have some reprogramming to do in your own software.

In this chapter, I am going to show you how to start working with your unconscious programming so you can change the results you are getting. The challenge, though, is that what is creating our results is in our unconscious, outside of our conscious awareness, so we have to learn ways to detect, find, and flush out what is there. We have to become good detectives to find what is happening within our inner programming that is creating the results we don't want.

In our unconscious, we have a number of different programs that are filtering the information and energy coming in through our five senses, creating our experience. These programs, which create our experience on the movie screen of our mind, are creating our behaviour, and our behaviour determines our results. One of those programs that is very easy to work with is our belief system. As we know, *what we believe is what we achieve.*

Three Steps to Change a Belief System

Step 1. Get clear on what it is you want to achieve in your life or in your specific area or context; e.g. sport, relationships, career, etc.

Step 2. Write down all limiting or negative beliefs within the unconscious in that specific context and get them on paper; e.g. Life is unfair.

Step 3. Reprogram yourself and install into the hard drive affirming, positive beliefs that are going to support you in creating the results you want in your life or that specific context; e.g. the flow of all good things comes to me easily and effortlessly.

Affirmations are a good way to start, but they take a long time to reprogram the unconscious mind. Below is an exercise on how you can find and change your beliefs in any area of your life quickly and effectively. The results are phenomenal because you are working directly with your hard drive and its programming to create different results.

Many people have completely turned their lives around, created the ideal partner, doubled their income, achieved their sporting goals, increased their performance – and I can speak to this from my own personal experience, through water-skiing, being in sales for Australia's number one personal development company, and running my own business. Working with my programming and upgrading it has massively supported me to achieve my goals in life.

Changing Your Beliefs

Step 1: What Do You Really Want?

Deepak Chopra teaches that it is important to take the time to sit in a quiet place, be still, and reflect on what you really want. In his training, 'The Soul of Leadership,' which I attended at the Kellogg School of Management, Northwestern University, Chicago, he teaches that great leaders ask great questions of themselves and others.

Ask yourself this question: "What do I really want?" It might be in a specific area of your life, or in general. What area of your life is not working as well as you would like it to? Take the time to reflect on what you really want to create in this area of your life. Pay attention to this question, "What do I really want?" and keep repeating it softly inside. Watch what arises from within, be present with what you become aware of, and then ask the question again. Keep repeating this until you are clear on what you want.

You can also ask yourself the following questions:

- If you had all the time and money in the world, what would you do?
- If you knew you couldn't fail, what would you do?
- If you had 12 months left to live, what would you do?

When this is clear, write it down.

Step 2: Finding Your Limiting Beliefs

Exercise 1.

What is it that prevents you from having what you want above? Why is that so? Why else? Write this down.

What excuses do you have that will stop you from getting what you want? Write them down.

What do you want but can't seem to achieve or do? Why is that? Write it down.

What do you want, but there is a lot of resistance or excuses stopping you from doing it? Write them down.

Exercise 2.

What patterns or results are you getting in your life, sport, career, etc., that you don't like, but they keep showing up, stopping you from getting what you want above? Write them down.

Looking at the list of patterns or results, choose one of the biggest reasons, the one that you think drives or creates the others in the list. Then ask yourself the following questions:

- *For what purpose do you think you are creating that result?* Why else? Write down your answers. Keep asking until you are empty, then read back what you have written down and ask the question again, writing down what comes up until you are empty.

- What do you believe about that specific result you are creating? What else do you believe? Write them down.

- What negative automatic thoughts come up inside regarding this result? Write them down.

- What things do you say to yourself that are negative or disempowering in regard to this result? Write them down.

Step 3: Reprogramming Your Hard Drive

Exercise 1.

Take your top three to six negative beliefs from Step 2, the three to six beliefs that are supporting and even creating most of the other beliefs you have written down.

Write them down in order of destructiveness, with the most disempowering destructive belief being first and so on. Next to that belief, write down the opposite, empowering, supporting, and positive belief.

Just in the act of becoming aware of your limiting programs, you can now make a change.

What you focus on is what you create. Look at your life today, and you will see what ou have been focusing on yesterday.

What will you choose to believe now? Why will you decide to believe that? Why else? Why else? Write down all the good benefits for why you now decide to choose that new empowering belief.

Exercise 2.

Now, remember a time when you were totally committed to a decision that you made that was very important. Remember a specific time, and go back to that time and see, hear, and feel how good it felt to feel that way.

Make that feeling even stronger now; hold your body in the way you did when you are totally committed to that something that is super important to you.

Holding onto this feeling, look at your new empowering belief and repeat the following statement: *"I am committed to*_____(your new belief)_____*because*_____(choose a benefit)_____*."*

Repeat the above with passion, either inside or out loud, allowing the feelings to strengthen within you. Each time you repeat it, choose a different benefit. Continue to repeat it and watch what happens to how you feel, how you move your body, and how you say this belief as it settles in and becomes a part of you.

How does this new belief make you feel?

What will this new belief support you in accomplishing

now?

Who is it that owns this new belief? Do you own it? Can anyone take that away from you?

Repeat this daily until you feel you have embodied it and it resonates with you inside.

Your internal programming is, in my opinion, the number one factor that determines your performance. Every breakthrough you have in your life starts with a change in your programming. You've got to align that inner game with your outer game and what you want to achieve.

To give an example of that, if you're a salesperson who wants to hit a certain income per year and you have the sales skills and can behave in the right way using those skills, but at the level of your beliefs, you believe it's difficult to make money or that money is the root of all evil, you're going to sabotage your success. You'll do well one

> **Purely from a mental perspective, the most important thing to work on is your internal programming. Change your programming, and you will change our results.**

month, and then you'll sabotage yourself with your beliefs

and your performance will drop, and you'll do poorly the next month. Our life circumstances and the results we get are created by our programming and reflect that directly.

Having worked with multinational companies and their leadership, I've clearly seen that when we work with their belief systems and inner game, setting that up for success, and aligning it with the company's goals, the leader moves into this place of doing less and achieving more. They're not struggling or swimming upstream to get to where they want to be, but they're actually going with the flow more and can tap into that flow, where everything happens easily and effortlessly.

Remember, we are unconscious of our programming because most of our programming is just that, unconscious. Our core values and beliefs are all set in the first 10 years of our life when we're imprinting everything, soaking it up like a sponge, mostly from our parents. The programming of a person is *everything*. If you don't

Change yourself and you literally change your world.

have that aligned with what you want, you're going to have a problem making it real in the world.

When you do get it right, or when you learn to make it

right, you can achieve anything you want. Really, the world is your oyster, and you can program yourself for success and truly achieve your goals and dreams. That's the consequence of doing this work. It's all good. If you work on yourself and grow, you change yourself and change your results.

If you learn how you work as a human being, if you learn some of the techniques to create change within the hard drive of your own computer, your own super-computer, you will be able to create the results that you really want. It's up to you.

There's a principle that Carl Jung, one of the leading psychologists in the first half of the 20ᵗʰ century, worked on: *everything that's out there is just a mirror reflection of what's going on inside here.* If you don't like the reflection that you're getting, don't point the finger and blame the reflection. You wouldn't do that if you were standing in front of a mirror and you didn't like the look of what you were wearing—no, you would go and change.

And that's the point. You can change, but people haven't been taught how, and that's what this book is about: empowering leadership and people to learn some of these powerful techniques so they can change their reflection.

The biggest challenge that the mind creates for us every day is to learn to discover what is programmed deep within ourselves that is creating our results. Now you have the answer. Just use your results as a mirror; they will tell you a lot about yourself and your internal programming.

The second biggest challenge is to get back in charge of your mind and its programming so it is not in charge of you. This you can do through controlling your attention, stopping stinking thinking, as well as changing your belief systems.

The third biggest challenge is to learn how to still our mind and eliminate the inner turbulence that comes from being out of balance. This we will get to in coming chapters.

The mind is just producing what it is programmed with over time. We must uncover the current limiting program-ming within our mind's matrix, which has come from so many years ago and is playing like a bad CD in our unconscious.

All is a reflection of your mind. Your mind and its programming make up the world. You don't see the world; you see your own self.

To achieve the above, my suggestion is to get passionate about discovering what is going on at an unconscious level within yourself and putting the techniques above into practice. Then you will liberate yourself from your limiting programming that no longer serves you. Are you in?

"Believing in negative thoughts is the single greatest obstruction to success."

~ **Charles F. Gassman**

2.

MASTERY OF YOUR EMOTIONS

"If I feel poverty, I will think of wealth to come.
If I feel incompetent, I will think of past success.
If I feel insignificant, I will remember my goals.
Today, I will be the master of my emotions."

~ **Og Mandino**

EMOTIONAL MASTERY IS essential for performing to your full potential and creating the results you want in life. Either you own your thoughts and emotions or they own you.

The essence is responsibility for our thoughts and emotions. If we fail to take responsibility, if we are unable to have the ability to respond, then we are at the whim of the world around us. Situations, circumstances, and people can push us around because they determine how we think and feel, not our own selves. Yes, we are literally owned by others; we are at the effect of the world and powerless to determine how we respond. People who live this way become very predictable, frustrated, blame the world, have plenty of excuses for not getting what they want, and the results they get in life are typically less than they expect or desire. To perform, to lead, to succeed, we must take full responsibility for our thoughts and feelings and for our focus and what we create in the world.

This chapter will support you in learning real-time

techniques that will teach you how to own, manage, and deal with your emotions so you will be able to stay in balance and choose how to respond according to the situation. This is choice, this is freedom, and this is personal power. When you are able to master this, you are able to behave in ways that will get better results and performance. Not only this, but you will live a more fulfilling life, choosing the best way to feel to get the result you want. Emotional mastery will support you in being all you can be, may it be so.

What is Emotional Mastery?

This next topic is extremely important when it comes to performing your best. It does not matter what field you are talking about; if you are not able to control and manage your emotions, you will not be able to control and manage your behaviour. All of your results are determined by your behaviour, and all of your behaviours are determined by your emotions. Emotional mastery is central to performing to your best consistently. You can have the most skilled person in their chosen endeavour, yet they can have severe performance

> **Emotional mastery is central to performing to your best consistently.**

anxiety. This typically means they are not able to get the best out of their skills and perform to their potential when it matters the most.

One day, I received a phone call from a cello player who had problems performing to his best in auditions. I heard him play his cello in the private surrounds of his own home, and his play was outstanding, mesmerizing. He explained that he could not play the same way when he was auditioning for a part in an orchestra because he was so nervous. I took him on as a client, and we began to work together.

In this case, this gentleman had no control over how he felt in a certain context. His emotions owned him, and he experienced extreme performance anxiety as if he had no control. No one else is responsible for how we feel; only we are, because we have a choice of how we want to feel. It is our responsibility to master our emotions and ours alone. The fact is that we have the choice to be able to feel what we want to feel, when we want to feel it.

What we don't own, owns us.

Our emotions are typically a product of our conditioning and are a reflection of the programming that is going on inside our unconscious mind. In fact, our unconscious is in charge of all of our emotions. Our emotions are a reflection of how we feel about certain people, situations, or circumstances in each moment. We emote. We do emotions. We feel. We're feeling creatures, emotional beings. We're not taught how to master our emotions, how to use our emotions to support us in achieving what we want. So it is that the majority of the population on this planet are at the effect of their emotions, projecting their unresolved issues into the world. They are owned by what they feel; and as a consequence, they are behaving based on these feelings. Consequently, we see so much violence and destruction in the world, which is just a reflection of the consciousness and feelings of the people involved in it.

What are Emotions?

For the sake of ease, let's say that emotions are either negative or positive. The negative ones tend to constrict us and limit us, and the positive ones tend to expand us and support us in achieving what we want. Essentially, emotions are energy in motion. An e-motion is energy that is in motion running through our body. We feel the emotion moving through us, and whether it is fear or whether it is happiness, every emotion has a beginning, middle, and an end. If we can remember this and let the energy flow, we can learn to master them. Then they become an amazing tool to support us in achieving what we dream of. The goal is to tame the energy and then channel it into the accomplishment of our purpose and goals.

Many people wonder where our emotions come from. Remember, they originate in the unconscious mind and are created due to the meanings we give to the world. We are meaning makers. There's no meaning out there—there are only the meanings that we give things. So the meaning that we attribute to certain situations, circumstances, and people creates our experiences or perception, which in turn determines the emotion that arises from within the unconscious. We don't have to think about which emotion we are going to feel—no, they arise unconsciously without even having to think about it. We could be sitting at home and the next minute we hear a scream from our partner, and a feeling of terror comes over us. The perception is that he is hurt. You run to him, and there he is, laughing at a naked neighbour who has locked himself outside. The unconscious mind thought it heard a distress signal from your partner, when what it really heard was a gasp of

> There's no meaning out there—there are only the meanings that we give things.

shock and surprise at seeing the neighbour outside trying to get in without being noticed.

So what is it that creates our unconscious perception and experiences, and how can we control our emotions when they are so unconscious and out of awareness?

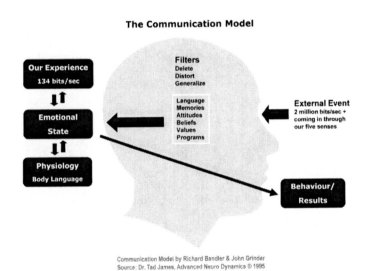

The Communication Model

Diagram: Communication Model from NLP

As you can see in the diagram above, our experience/perception is created by our filters: our belief systems, our values, our human needs, our internal programs, and even our vision and purpose. All of this creates our perception of what's happening.

For example, several people can go to the same movie, but each person has a different perception and experience of that movie. Some may decide they like the movie and some don't. We all create our own perception, because the filters that create it inside our unconscious mind are full of different content according to our life experiences and how we were programmed when we were growing up. There are just as many worlds in this world as there are people, because we all have our own model of the world or mental matrix. Everyone's programmed and conditioned differently.

Emotions Affect Performance

Negative emotions or being in a negative state causes us to actually behave poorly, and that's very easily seen in sport. When an athlete gets into a negative state, they lose confidence, they drop their head, their body changes, and then they start to play poorly. It is also the same in different roles and situations, whether as a parent at home or a leader in the office—our state determines how we behave, and our behaviour then determines the results that we're going to get.

We are responsible for our thoughts and feelings. Our emotions are very much a product of our thoughts inside. It is super-important that we actually learn how to stay in charge of our emotions and not let them take over us. To learn how to work with them so we stay resourceful and behave in the way that we want to behave to attain our goals and perform to our best.

Owning Our Emotions

Emotional control is important. Athletes are a great example. If you look at some of the best athletes in the world, they are very good at controlling their emotions.

One example of an emotional meltdown was when Andy Murray played Grigor Dimitrov in the quarterfinals of Wimbledon in 2014, just one year after Murray won the title. He lost in straight sets 6-1, 7-6, 6-2 in just under two hours. Murray was in such a state on the tennis court that he wasn't even in the game. Dimitrov, on the other hand, was steely and never showed emotion. He never showed any self-criticism toward himself, and he was totally on fire and performing to his best.

Learning how to control our emotions will give us the best performance. If we don't, we're out of control, which will not lead to great performance. Learning to master our emotions and channel them correctly will give us the freedom to be present. This is the place where all good things are created from.

We are responsible for our thoughts and feelings.

Not controlling our emotions on the other hand is not having the ability to take responsibility and to creatively respond to situations and circumstances. We are essentially allowing people to push us around emotionally, which will lead us to being reactive to people, situations, and circumstances, instead of responding creatively.

In his book, *The 7 Habits of Highly Effective People*, Stephen Covey reminds us of Pavlov's experiment with his dog. With food, he provided a stimulus and rang a bell to anchor the bell to the stimulus or food. Eventually, all he had to do was ring the bell and the dog would salivate—stimulus—response. If the stimulus and response are very close to each other, it means that we're just reacting to a stimulus and we're owned by that stimulus. There are a lot of examples like this in everyday life. We meet an angry person and get angry ourselves, or our alarm going off means get up, or seeing the TV means turn it on. The truth is we have a choice; we can stretch that gap between stimulus and response to make it nice and wide and choose what to do.

Choice is very empowering. We want the ability to be able to creatively choose. Instead of it being stimulus–response, it's stimulus; we enter the gap and are able to respond creatively. We own our emotions if we have the ability to respond to situations, circumstances, and people. *We* decide how we feel and behave, and how it is best to feel, to support us in achieving our goals.

Diagram: Stimulus Response with choice

Choice

Goals | Creativity

Stimulus → | **Response**

Values | Presence

By: Victor E. Frankl

We need to build that muscle within ourselves and practice. We need to become aware of when we are reacting and when the stimulus response is very quick. We need to apply certain techniques to stay in charge of our emotions so we can perform to our best and avoid losing control of them. Living in the Bahamas, I see in the culture here examples of people who lose control all of the time. The newspapers are full of stories about people

Freedom is one of the highest values of human beings.

who have moments of insanity and behave in ways they regret for the rest of their lives. The media in America presents examples of police officers that lose control and make silly decisions in the heat of the moment. Professional athletes who lose control of their emotions get banned from playing their chosen sport because they were irresponsible with the people they love the most. It is rife throughout society and the cause of all the violence that we see in this modern day and age.

Learn to Control

There are a number of things we can do to control our emotions.

1. The first thing is to own our emotions and be 100% responsible for them. In the context of the inner game, being our thoughts and feelings, it is important that we *fully own* and take responsibility for our emotions. No excuses—you own them, they are yours, and no one makes you feel anything—you do.

   Only we are responsible for how we think and feel. Taking full ownership and responsibility will give us the power to decide, creating personal freedom.

2. The second thing people need to learn is to control emotions. The tool that will get you in charge is to use your breath. Your breath is linked to your

emotions. The deeper and lower in the belly you breathe, the calmer you will become.

As an example, at my first World Championships in 1988 in Melbourne, Australia, I was standing on the river bank preparing for my turn to get in the water. It was quite an accomplishment that I made the finals in the jump event at my first world titles. I was only 18 years of age and competing with the top 12 jumpers in the world. Some of them were my heroes, people I had looked up to and wanted to emulate for years.

I was *so* nervous—my anxiety started to overcome me. John Pennay, future world champion, who was competing for Australia and had been working with the Australian Institute of Sport and their team of sports psychologists noticed my state and offered to help me calm my nerves. He taught me a technique called belly breathing, which I still use to this day to calm myself when I need to. It will calm your mind, your thoughts, and your feelings.

This technique uses your breath to move that energy through your body and stops it from getting stuck. If we stop breathing, the energy will stop moving and we will continue to feel our anxiety. Use your breath to move your emotion through your body. Please pass this technique on to your children and people you love.

3. The third way to control your emotions is to use your conscious mind to focus on what it is you want to achieve and not on what you *don't* want. What we focus on is what we create. Thinking incorrectly and seeing yourself fail is going to create anxiety, nervousness, etc. Use your mind correctly. Nervousness and anxiety are big problems that stop people from performing at their best because they allow their thoughts to be focused on negative things happening in the future.

Consciously focus on what you want and use your mind proactively to visualize and feel how good it feels when you achieve it. Visualization is a powerful tool to support you in staying in charge of your emotions and program yourself for success.

Here are three interesting techniques on how to visualize.

1. Get very clear about what you want and write it down as if you've already got it.

2. Come to a specific place, a nice and quiet place, and sit down and actually take two or three minutes to

see that through your own eyes. Visualize yourself achieving what it is you want to achieve, looking through your own eyes. See yourself doing what you want to do, then tap into the feelings of how good that feels.

3. When feeling really positive and really good inside, make that feeling as strong as possible and put that into your fist. Squeeze your hand and put it all in there and put all those positive feelings into your hand. That creates a trigger, and a trigger is great, because it creates a positive resource so when you become unresourceful and start to feel negative, you can just squeeze your hand and all those positive feelings come up, which will help you control your emotions.

Your Physiology

The field of Cognitive Behavioural Sciences, contributed to by John Grinder and Richard Bandler with the founding of Neuro Linguistic Programming, discovered the power of our physiology. *Physiology is another* way we can learn to control our emotions. How we hold our body determines how we feel. If we want to feel confident, we stand confidently and behave confidently. If we want to feel happy, we show the face of happiness. We can use our body consciously to tap into how we feel. When we're totally in charge of our feelings, there are no excuses anymore. We decide how it's best to feel to support getting the specific result we want to get.

If you've got a very important meeting you need to perform very well in, I recommend that you tap into a time when you had the best meeting of your life. Remember that time and feel how good it felt in the meeting to be on fire. Move your body in the way you want to feel: confident, powerful, and expressive. Walk into the meeting and stay that way throughout the meeting. You will get a different result compared to being in an unresourceful state, feeling insecure and unconfident.

Fight/Flight Response

The fight/flight response is a stress response. The reptilian brain is the oldest part of the brain, which is in charge of the fight/flight response. What tends to happen when we're under stress and the fight/flight response kicks in, is that the blood gets redirected to our muscles, adrenalin starts to pump through our veins, and the body prepares to fight or run for its life. We become

> **How we hold our body determines how we feel.**

much more reactive, rather than responsive. We are not making an effective judgment call, using the forebrain or the neo-cortex to make rational decisions.

Often when we are under high stress, we become irrational, and that can be useful in some situations, but it can be problematic, especially in relationships or work situations. When the unconscious mind is feeling threatened, the reptilian brain kicks in; it is a survival mechanism. Everyone has it, and it is needed.

We need to learn how to switch off the fight/flight response and also learn what is it that actually triggers the fight/flight response in modern-day society. This old brain of ours is not really designed to handle this modern-day way of life. In the past, we would see a lion. The lion would chase us—fight/flight would come in, and we'd go into survival mechanism. Now, we drink a cup of coffee, fight/flight kicks in, and we get all stressed. We get into an argument with our colleague from work, and we move into fight/flight. Many people are so high strung that the fight/flight response is kicking in far too much and too often. Fight/Flight response happens in reaction to any stressor—not just things that we would see as particularly stressful, but minute things, like having a slight intolerance to foods or having various aches and pains around the body. It's a cumulative effect. It's that awareness that you may have had no major stresses in your life, but if you've got 10 minor stresses, it adds up to a big stress.

The secret for mastering the fight/flight response is to learn techniques to switch that off and control your emotions and what they trigger. A typical mistake people make is that they hold their breath. Basically, when we move into a stress response, people constrict and tighten up, and the breathing starts to become shallower. We breathe from the top of our lungs, which then really starts to trigger the sympathetic nervous system. Then our blood supply changes and moves to the muscles. There's an automatic response that starts to happen. If people are not conscious, not aware, and don't know how to deal with that, they just get caught up in a negative loop and reacting.

Other typical mistakes are people talk negatively to themselves or blame themselves or others. It creates a downward spiral in cognition, where they basically become very unresourceful with their thoughts and then very unresourceful with their emotions. Their behaviour will change, and their results change with it. One of the most important things to do is to support people in learning specific techniques to overcome these challenges—how to get back in charge when they seem to be out of control and how to give them choices so they can respond creatively.

People with High Emotional Mastery

People who are highly responsible and have the ability to respond are able to stay calm under pressure. They are the type of people who are not moving into the fight/flight response when the pressure comes on. They're able to think clearly, respond creatively, communicate effectively, and behave appropriately in accordance with how they need to behave to achieve the result that they want.

This is a real skill. This is something that we can learn, but it takes time, and we have to practice this over time so we can build up our emotional muscles. Athletes and people who are conscious of their health go to the gym every day and start to build up their muscles physically to be stronger and condition themselves. We also need to consider that we need to build up our emotional muscles, our emotional strength, and that conditioning, as well.

In his book, *Legacy*, James Kerr talks about the New Zealand All Black rugby team and how they cracked under pressure when playing France on two separate occasions at two separate World Cups. Before the World Cup in New Zealand in 2011, the New Zealanders made the decision to train themselves in the skill to learn to stay cool, calm, and present when the pressure came on. The All Blacks made the final that year and played against their arch enemy, France. When the pressure came on, their training came into play, and they were able to make the right decisions and stay present in the now. The result being New Zealand took the win 8-7 in the closest fought World Cup final on record.

The consequence of not mastering our emotions is that nothing's going to change. Are we at the effect of other people, or are we the ones who are at cause and responsible for how we feel? If we don't find the answer to this question, we're going to be very easily pushed around by others our whole life. Other people will determine our feelings, and we'll be on an emotional roller-coaster ride. We've got to get people back in charge, back in that driver's seat, and support others and ourselves in mastering our emotions so that we can perform, have a better quality of life, and enjoy the journey— because that's the point. The next moment's not guaranteed, and the goal is to enjoy our life as much as possible—

> The next moment's not guaranteed, and the goal is to enjoy our life as much as possible— emotional mastery supports us in doing that.

emotional mastery supports us in doing that. Who can you share this with today to help them increase the quality of their life and make a difference?

"A man who is master of himself can end a sorrow as easily as a pleasure. I don't want to be at the mercy of my emotions. I want to use them, enjoy them, and dominate them."

~ Oscar Wilde

3.

MASTERY OF YOUR BODY

"Sleep is the golden chain that ties health and our bodies together."

~ Thomas Dekker

The Benefits of a Healthy Lifestyle

BY BEING HEALTHY, you will have better concentration levels, more energy, better work output, more enthusiasm, and a better quality of life. Whether you're the boss looking for better results from your staff or you're an employee working diligently to get a raise or promotion, if you look after yourself from a nutritional perspective, from a movement perspective, and from a sleep perspective and make sure that what you're doing is in alignment with your goals, you can only expect the results to be great and fulfilling.

In this chapter, you will learn serious tips on how to look after yourself. A lot of people haven't learned how to look after themselves. They haven't gone to courses to learn how to master themselves physically. But when you apply the techniques and tips discussed in this chapter to your life, you'll have good health and great performance in the weeks, months, and years ahead.

A *Healthy Person* Defined

The traditional definition of a healthy person is a person without disease. I have a different perspective. A healthy person is a human being who is whole, physically active, and healed. A whole person is a person made up of mind, body, and spirit. It's someone who has high IQ and is applying that to themselves. It is someone who has a high EQ, emotional intelligence, and they're able to do that. It may also be someone who doesn't necessarily have a high IQ, but has had great conditioning in the past and a great childhood with supportive, loving, trusting, positively encouraging, unconditional parents. I think that's a very important factor—the conditioning of the parents and the family impact on health and the healthy person.

A healthy mind is one that has had positive, affirming experiences in the past; has positive programming; has no significant trauma in the past that is holding them back or is causing problems in the unconscious; has great relationships and a support network around them on the social side.

> A healthy person is one that has had positive, affirming experiences in the past.

A healthy person is someone who is physically robust and has a healthy immune system, someone who is conscious of what type of fuel to put in their body that is right for them. It is someone who is moving on a regular basis, someone who is lifting and strengthening their system, and someone who is stable emotionally and empathetic.

As a top performance consultant, when working with athletes in the past, a number of aspects contribute to high performance: the athlete's technical ability, their tactical skills, mental strength and emotional control, physical health, and also the social impact of the people around them.

A healthy person has a very good balance between all of these aspects and has a level of mastery in all of these areas as well. From the perspective of a healthy person and the definition given earlier, I think they have a much higher chance of performing to their potential than someone who is not well-balanced, who is not what I described earlier, and is perhaps the opposite, because of how they're programmed and the challenges that they'll be facing because of that.

My Journey of Health

Personally, as someone who is paid to deliver and

perform and help others to perform to their potential, it's important to walk the talk and put into practice what you've learned.

It wasn't until I started to have some quite serious symptoms in my body that I understood how powerful our health is in regard to impacting our performance. I had unexplained knee swelling, aches, and pains in my body and trouble staying focused at work, all while eating well, exercising, and living a healthy lifestyle. After I started to experience these symptoms, my performance started to deteriorate. I wasn't working effectively. I wasn't able to play with my sons the same way I had or play sport.

Following my principle of *if you want to be the best, go and hang out with the best,* I looked up an old colleague who is one of the best in Europe at treating people and their health issues, a gentleman named Matt Walden from Primal Lifestyle in Surrey. He supported me in assessing the challenges that I was experiencing. In the process, we discovered that I was intolerant to certain foods. This intolerance was causing a serious immune response, which was causing certain symptoms, aches and pains, and digestive

What you look after, looks after you.

challenges, amongst swelling, switching off certain muscles in the body, etc., etc. I didn't understand that what we eat can totally determine the health of our physiology and our immune system and affect it so powerfully. It was through learning from Matt about my metabolic type or how my body is designed to metabolize food that I discovered it was best for me was to eat gluten-free, organic only, limiting dairy products, grains, and alcohol consumption. By applying his recommendations, I started to turn things around and am now much healthier and happier.

The Top 5 Health Challenges of the 21st Century

From a health perspective, the top five performance detractors are:

1. **Negative Stress**—is often the root cause of problems with health. It comes in many shapes and sizes from physical and mental to nutritional and chemical. There are internal and external stressors; and when they accumulate over time in your nervous system, they start to add up. The more stress you experience, the more stress hormones you produce, and your body starts to break down.

2. **Lack of sleep**—One of the biggest challenges that people face is switching off at night and getting to bed. For thousands of years, we have lived in

harmony with the day and night cycles, driven by the sun. Nowadays, we have bright lights in the evening causing our "active" hormone or cortisol to stay elevated in our bodies far too long, interrupting our rest and recovery time at night. This has disastrous effects on the physiology.

3. **Eating the wrong type of food**—Most people don't understand what sort of fuel to put into their body to support them in performing to their full potential, and it's causing stress. A major part of this is actually dehydration. Most people drink too many diuretics, too much coffee, and/or too much alcohol and become dehydrated without knowing it.

4. **Inability to "pause"**—During this age of global reach due to the Internet, the majority of the population, including children, choose not to "switch off" their mind and allow it to continue working at home or after their daily activities.

5. **Deterioration of relationships**—As people strive for success, they lose balance and lose touch with themselves; therefore, they lose touch with the people they love the most. This affects people's stress and health and is a major concern for some of the clients I've worked with.

The Reality of the Corporate World

Almost all of the business corporations I've worked with are challenged to find the balance between getting results and the well-being of their human capital or staff. They are so focused on external results that their leadership has not learned the science of performance from a health perspective. They are ignorant to the fact that the overall health of their staff affects the performance of their company, including engagement levels, the turnover of valuable people in the business, and the numbers of burnout cases. All these issues add up to costing companies literally *millions and millions* of dollars every year, and the GDP of nations' economies *billions* of dollars yearly.

It's definitely time that the corporate world wakes up to the fact that they need to work with their staff as whole people. The company's greatest asset and largest investment should be their primary concern to support performing to their full potential. It is well overdue for leadership to begin to understand how health drives performance. At the moment, leadership is too fixated on getting the external results and giving external support. They pay for gym memberships, massages, and activities, but they're not really dealing with the inner game of health, as I'd like to call it. They're aware of the outer effects of it, but they haven't gotten to the cause and started to work with it—because they don't know how. I see that as a *major* gap in the corporate world that needs to be addressed, and we're touching on this—just touching on it—to help create awareness in these pages.

Whoever you are and wherever you come from, if you're a human being, your health affects you, whether you like it or not. Health *has* to be our number one value. If we don't have health, we have nothing—we have no quality of life. It has to become a priority for every person in this world, and we need to wake up, because the number one killer in the western world is heart disease. Yet, over 100 years ago, heart disease didn't exist. Before 1900, pneumonia was the biggest killer in the USA and life expectancy was 47 years old. By 1930, after years of medical research into fighting infectious diseases, pneumonia was eradicated and heart disease became number one. What has happened in the last 100 years that is causing literally millions of people on this planet to die every year from coronary heart disease? It's time to wake up.

> **Health has to be our number one value. If we don't have health, we have nothing—we have no quality of life.**

An *Unhealthy Person* Defined

An unhealthy person is a human being who's off-purpose with what they believe they're here to do or, indeed, don't know what they're here to do. As a result, they are drifting—not just in their general behaviours, but in their health and lifestyle behaviours, as well. They're really allowing themselves to be influenced by commercial advertising and what their tribe is doing.

A major influencer for unhealthy people is the pressure from the community to conform to unhealthy habits. An example of this at the moment is the population of the western world, where an unhealthy lifestyle is prevalent, resulting in obesity, diabetes, heart disease, and cancer at rates that are unprecedented. As such, we realize that the majority of communities globally are not moving forward toward a healthy, happy, and fulfilling existence where they can realize their potential as human beings.

It's essential to get clear and focused on what your goals, dreams, and legacy are, in order to become informed about your lifestyle, nutrition, and exercise choices and provide some of that motivation to break away from the pack on those fronts. This is not to be isolated, but to lead the way, to become leaders within the community in whatever form that it takes for you, as an individual.

This leads to the fact that purpose equals performance. Knowing what your purpose is and why you are here, what you're good at, what you love to do, how to contribute to others using your talents and abilities, and being true to that is a major contribution to top performance. Those people who are performing to their potential are *very* clear on why they're here and what their purpose is, and work is a vocation. It's not a job. It's something they love to do, so they're very much in the present moment, enjoying the present moment of what they're doing. They're *being* more and fulfilling more of their potential. They're much happier, as well, and a happy person contributes to a healthy person, high performance, and happy customers.

Paul Chek's Four Doctors

Paul Chek is the author of the book *Eat, Move and Be Healthy* and is a colleague of Matthew Wallden. In fact, Matthew is one of a few people on the Chek Institute's faculty team. In his book, he talks about four different doctors who are the last doctors you'll ever need. The concept is that you need to consult with them to get things right and get your health optimized.

Dr. Happiness

The doctor who guides you to a healthy space through contemplation and planning about why you exist—to establish what your goals, dreams, and legacy really are. This information is actually important to the other three doctors. So, once you know what Dr. Happiness has to tell you, you can really create an effective health plan with Dr. Diet, Dr. Quiet, and Dr. Movement.

Dr. Diet

We are what we eat. Proper nutrition is extremely important. You've *got* to find out your metabolic type and how your nervous system's blueprint is designed so you can fuel it correctly. For example, if you're putting diesel into a petrol car, it's not going to operate. It's the same with us. Some of us run on CNG; some of us run on diesel; some of us are running on petrol, etc. As such, we want to find out the ideal fuel type for us and feed that to ourselves in the right percentage and combination of carbohydrates, fats, and proteins.

Furthermore, when we eat is another issue. We're not just what we eat, we are also when we eat. We need to take that knowledge and apply it by eating at the right times, eating in the right way with the right food, and consuming the right liquids to stay hydrated. It's vital for top performance.

Dr. Movement

First and foremost, you need to be aware of the current

situation of your body, i.e. what muscles are tight, what muscles are loose, etc. Then, begin an exercise regime that is designed to bring those muscles into positive balance. Your nervous system, skeletal system, and muscular system need to be strengthened in a specific way that's tailored to you. There's no health program that fits everyone. Everyone is unique. Everyone has a different history. Therefore, their body reflects that uniqueness, and there is a bespoke need and design applied to each person.

Dr. Quiet

The least understood of the four doctors is Dr. Quiet. I'm going to spend more time with this doctor, because it doesn't get enough attention. People don't know how to deal with Dr. Quiet because, if we trace this problem back to its cause, we can see people don't have a clear idea what their goals, dreams, and legacy are and how to get there. Figuratively speaking, most people generate the burning desire to, let's say, run a marathon, join an iron man contest, or climb a mountain. Unfortunately, they tend to just go and start climbing. They just climb and climb until they run

> There's no health program that fits everyone. Everyone is unique.

out of energy and fall asleep. Guess what? They are going to die when they fall off the mountain. If you run until you can't run anymore, you're going to get injured or not come out of it very well. The point is whenever you have a dream, ambition, goal, or legacy you want to leave behind, it's essential also to be aware and understand how to manage yourself to achieve that end result. That's where Dr. Quiet comes in.

Dr. Quiet is often overlooked, unlike the other doctors—especially Dr. Movement and Dr. Diet, who receive a bit more attention, i.e. we decide to go to the gym and create New Year's resolutions, like cutting out sugar or following a special diet.

How do we effectively deal with Dr. Quiet? Practice being silent. On a daily basis, have downtime and take a little sabbatical to slow down and become still. That means not reading a book, not listening to any music, but instead being out in nature and listening to the sounds, or sitting still, being present and focusing on your breathing. Meditating or just being quiet on a regular basis

On a daily basis, have downtime and take a little sabbatical to slow down and become still.

allows your nervous system to come into balance. In turn, your consciousness comes into balance, which will support Dr. Happiness in really kicking in. When you're able to be present and take the time to be in the now, you experience within yourself joy, happiness, and fulfilment. Positive emotions arise from within when you take the time to be quiet and still.

A little disclaimer here: this does not happen immediately, but over time. The deeper we become present, the more happiness and joy starts to prevail in our consciousness.

The Don't Do List

Consistently, avoid specific things that are detrimental to the human physiology on certain levels, i.e. smoking, tobacco, drinking alcohol, etc. There are certain things that have a detrimental effect to our health and well-being and are literally toxic. Unfortunately, not doing some of them may potentially have a psychological, emotional, or social impact, as well. As such, there's always a balance to be struck between things that are nutritionally or biochemically bad for us and things that may also have an emotional benefit of some sort. The optimal thing is to get into balance and minimize the things that stress us, i.e. minimize drinking coffee and alcohol, smoking tobacco, while optimizing and maximizing our intake of water, organic fruits and vegetables, high quality meats, and so on.

Sharing these secrets in these pages is going to make a massive difference to you as the information will help you create physical mastery, which will in turn support you in achieving top performance on a daily basis.

To be a top-class athlete, you have to train hard, you have to eat right, and you have to get enough rest. You have to treat yourself as an athlete."

~ Rory McIlory

4.

HOW TO PERFORM
OUT OF YOUR MIND

"Let your performance do the thinking."

~ H. Jackson Brown, Jr.

A NO-MIND EXPERIENCE is a phenomenon that people experience when their mind is completely still. In this state, they have no internal dialogue running, and they are externally focused on the job at hand. Due to there being no thoughts, there is nothing but the experience of the now or present moment. Here, people feel fulfilled, at peace, content. They are able to perform at high levels under intense pressure, often breaking their own or others' records. They make great decisions, conserve energy, and have peak experiences where they perceive that time slows down, that they are moving in slow motion, and that there is no effort in what they are doing. From the observer's perspective, everything seems to be achieved so easily when seeing this person in action. Their performance is graceful and mesmerizing. This experience is not experienced all of the time by the person; it comes and goes and is ephemeral. The person who is lucky to experience this wants more, yet the more they want it, the less the chance they will experience it again. It is not something that they achieve; it comes to them when they let go and least expect it.

Wouldn't you agree there is no better place to be? It sounds absolutely wonderful to be in this place. To be in the "flow" or the "zone" is to be able to perform at the peak of your mental and physical capabilities. It is every athlete's dream to be able to tap into this at will. Psychology says that it can't be created at will and that you will be lucky to experience this more than a handful of times in a career. This is the case with the majority of people, but there are a few who have learned to break through and switch this on at will. Having studied the "no-mind" experience for the last 20 years, I am happy to say that there is a way to tap into the "zone" at will, and in the coming pages, I am going to show you how so you can perform to your potential when it matters the most.

There is a term called "getting out of your own way." What does it mean exactly when one "gets out of their own way?" This statement refers to having a no-mind experience. There are no negative thoughts or feelings. There is just a still mind focused on the task at hand, allowing the body to do what it was trained to do, perform! We've spent a lot of time talking about the mind and emotions, and now we are going to talk about what happens when we train ourselves to switch off the thinking and feeling and enter into the world of no mind.

When I was an athlete, barefoot water-skiing for New Zealand, I had a number of experiences where I was able to perform to my full potential and basically had what is called a peak experience. There was no thinking; there was no struggling; there was no effort—there was just a flow of performance. It was effortless, and I broke personal bests in those moments. I was curious: what was that all about? What was that experience? That doesn't happen all of the time, but when it does, it's really great, and I want more of that. So I started asking other athletes I knew—what were you thinking about when you broke that world record or achieved a personal best? And they all told me, "Nothing – I'm not thinking anything." This confirmed my own experience, and after reflecting on my findings, I realized that *not thinking* was a good thing—that learning to switch off thoughts before, during, and after a performance was critical for success. Earlier in my career, I had learned that my thoughts affect my behaviour, which affects my results. This was taking things to a whole new level. I was learning to not think at all.

After more investigation, I found that there's a whole science around "the flow" – which is also called "the zone." When athletes and people tap into the zone, they perform literally out of their mind. I've heard a lot of athletes say, "Oh, I performed so well. I performed out of my mind today." What does that actually mean? Well, it means that they had a "no mind" experience. When athletes or people perform to their best, they are not trying—there's no effort—and they are getting out of their own way. Their mind has been put aside and transcended even, and they are entering into a space where they operate at a higher level and peak performance is achieved.

It's all a matter of quieting your thoughts, stilling your mind, and fully coming into the present. The key is to be able to do this in the midst of dynamic activity and maintain it. Easier said than done, but when achieved, well worth it— well worth it, indeed. I will attempt to keep this as simple as possible and share some 'how to' exercises that, when put into practice, will support you in peaking and attaining top performance.

It's a matter of quieting your thoughts, stilling your mind, and fully coming into the present.

To Mind or Not to Mind, That is the Question

I made it my purpose to start to really find out how I had that peak experience. What I learned took me deep into the depth of the mind and the human soul in order to understand how to replicate that performance and experience. What I found changed my life forever and supported me in getting to where I am today.

The mind is made up of conscious and unconscious thinking, and its momentum is huge. It likes to stay in charge, to control situations, circumstances, and people, and run the game of life. Our conditioning and our programming, all stored in the unconscious mind, are the source of our focus and thinking. Between all of our thoughts, emotions, and underlying conditioning, we have so much to manage and deal with it sometimes can become overwhelming. To be able to learn to still that mind and really put it aside is a great skill, and, in my opinion, is actually *the* number one skill that anyone who wants to perform highly needs to learn.

Let's take a look at the top three reasons why people should learn to still their mind.

1. The mind with its negative programming can get in the way, and it can sabotage us and our results. So if we can learn to transcend it and still it completely, that programming will not affect us anymore.

2. Our thoughts and emotions, if they're unresourceful, create stress, and stress *kills* performance. The

higher the level of negative stress, the lower the level of performance. Refer to the following diagram.

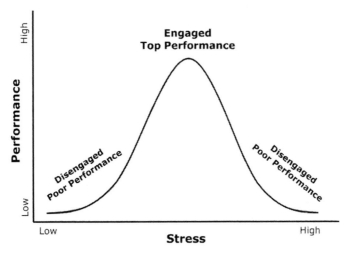

Yerkes-Dodson Human Performance and Stress Curve

Diagram of Stress vs Performance

3. When our mind is still and we are in the present, it creates a lot of flow in our life, and things happen without effort. Bruce Lee mentioned that the more relaxed you are, the faster you can strike or the harder you can hit. Sprinters who tighten up at the end of the 100 meters are the ones that start to slow down, and the ones who are able to let go and relax through the last 20 meters of the race are the ones who keep top speed.

How can we stay calm and relaxed to allow top performance to occur? Well, we have to learn to get out of the way of our own selves and master our mind.

The Challenge

If we haven't taken the time to be still on a regular basis, then we have so much momentum in our thinking that when we sit down and try to be still, we find our thoughts just continue automatically in the background. This is called inner turbulence, and in everyday life, we aren't aware of it because it's in the background all of the time.

This inner turbulence is an example of a mind not being still or of us getting in the way of our own self. It's this inner turbulence that is actually stopping us from getting out of our own way and performing to our full potential. We have to learn to still the mind and switch it off, and this is a major challenge if we have been taught all of our life to *do* and not to just be. This happens because these techniques are not taught to us as children—

The challenge is clear, the challenge is achievable, and like any challenge, it takes commitment and desire to accomplish it. .

they are not taught to us, period. We have to look for those answers by becoming aware of problems and how to overcome those problems.

The challenge is clear, the challenge is achievable, and like any challenge, it takes commitment and desire to accomplish it. You have to make it, for a period of time, the most important focus in your life. Most importantly, you need to understand why that is the case. Why do you want that? How will that support you? What will happen if you don't do it? Do you want that? Ask yourself those big questions and find out your big reasons for doing it, because when it gets tough, and it will, you want to be able to remember what the purpose of all this was in the first place.

Who am I?

The question arises, if I want to still my mind and switch it off, then what is left? Who am I with no mind? Will I drop dead when my mind stops? What is it that is running my body? These questions point to the very nature of who we are. Deepak Chopra talks about the three big questions that need answering by each and every one of us: "Who am I?," Why am I here?" and "What do I really want?" The answers, when found upon reflection, are very liberating. Let's see if we can discover them together below.

It is clear that when an athlete or person in the midst of dynamic activity has the fortune to be in the place where stillness within is experienced and the mind has switched off, they don't drop dead due to not having any thoughts. Plainly and obviously, we are not our thoughts—we are more than our thoughts. Are we just a body then? Quantum physics has discovered that the physical world is made of atoms and subatomic particles. That in fact, everything is just energy and information. Not only is it energy and information, it is thinking energy and information. It has a consciousness to it. This is called the quantum field in scientific terms. You physical body is part of this field, and this field is the consciousness upon which all of existence in the physical world is founded. This same force grows your body from two cells in the womb to a three to four trillion cell highly conscious being in adulthood.

So if we're not our thoughts, then who are we? If the body and mind are the hardware, the hard drive and the software, who is the operator? The operator is this powerful force found in the silence between our thoughts. The consciousness, which runs our mind and body, is the operator of the computer. Even when we're deep asleep, we're still conscious. There is a self, a consciousness that is aware when someone walks in the room—it's pure awareness. That awareness is there. It's this consciousness which we want to actually tap into, and we can only tap into that when we get out of the way of ourselves and learn how to still our mind. This powerful force that is who we are is not found in our mind or thoughts, it is found in the gap between our thoughts, in the no mind.

Who are you? You are that force which is the thinker of the thoughts, breather of the breath, beater of the heart, and seer of the scenery. You are that which animates the mind and body and is also beyond it all. When you become still inside, you transcend the operating equipment and become one with the user. This is the secret of the sages, an ageless force of nature; your own soul, which when tapped into directly, allows you to experience who you really are, powerful and unlimited. Who you are is beyond the mind and body.

In the East, they have known this for millennia. In all the cultures across the world, they have different names for the same source. In India, it is Brahman; in China, it is Tao; in Native America, it is Great Spirit or Great Mystery. In psychology, they call it "the super conscious mind" which transcends the conscious and unconscious/subconscious minds. So in many different cultures, across many different centuries, everyone is aware of this third self that is your full potential, which when you tap into it, you have a peak experience and perform to your full potential.

Below you can see a diagram of how Dr. Tad James and Michelle Duval describe what in religion is called The Holy Trinity.

- The conscious mind acts as the loving parent or *Father*.

- The subconscious mind acts as the innocent child or *Son*.

- The super conscious mind acts as the *Holy Spirit*.

The Whole of You

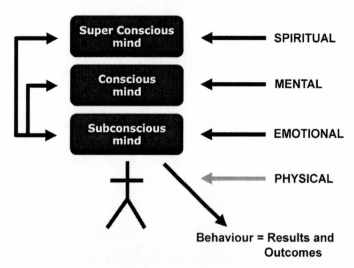

By Michelle Duval, Equilibrio © 2005

How to Still Your Mind

"Lose your mind and come to your senses."

~ Fritz Perls

This is where the rubber hits the road. The application of tried and tested tools will help you still your mind and tap into your potential on a daily basis. I am going to share with you three practices that will support you in connecting with the silence within.

Taking the Time to Be

The number one thing people can do on a regular basis to switch off the mind is to learn to just be. To give ourselves the opportunity to just "be" on a regular basis and as human beings connect with our true nature, supports us in coming back into balance and performing to our best. It is in our nature to excel, to strive, and to perform. The human being is, in fact, designed to do so. The problem is human beings have become human doings and lost touch with their true nature and all the benefits that come with it. Joy, fulfilment, a meaningful existence, peak performance, and

The number one thing people can do on a regular basis to switch off the mind is to learn to just be.

optimum health are all our birthrights, to name just a few. So how do we just "be," and what does that entail?

Most commonly described as meditation, taking the time to "be" has been recognized by the scientific community and more recently the business community as being one of the most important methodologies, if not *the* most important methodology, to increase performance.

Following are a few benefits that come from taking the time to just "be" on a daily basis that I learned from Dr. Deepak Chopra when I did his Primordial Sound Meditation course in 1996.

Scientific studies done on meditation over two decades have proven that:

1. Meditation directly releases stress.

2. Long-term meditators are much more able to cope with stress.

3. People who meditate can go into a relaxing state, twice as deep as deep sleep. This can happen in ten minutes, compared to four to six hours when we are sleeping.

4. Biological age is reversed through meditation. Robert Wallace at UCLA, California, found that people who have meditated for five years or more have a biological age on average 12 years younger

than their actual age.

5. Our health improves. A health study done on a group of 2,000 people who meditate showed that they were hospitalized for heart disease 87% less often than non-meditators, and were hospitalized 50% less often for cancer. The people were also much healthier than the average population in 17 major areas of serious disease, both mental and physical.

6. Meditation improves our ability to focus, our creativity, learning ability, and memory.

7. Meditation creates more harmony and gives us more energy and a deep sense of fulfilment in our lives.

8. Meditation supports us in coming into the "now" and staying present in the midst of dynamic activity, where peak performance comes from.

How to Just "Be"

Learning to meditate, or in other words, learning to still your mind, is recommended in the following ways. I do recommend learning to meditate from a registered trainer from the following schools: "Primordial Sound Meditation" or "Transcendental Meditation." The reason being is that through immersing yourself in the weekend course, you will learn the philosophy, as well as receive a mantra designed for you that supports you in stilling your mind rapidly. Here are some helpful tips from studying Primordial Sound Meditation with Dr. Deepak Chopra in 1996, that will help you make a start today.

There are three experiences that can happen when you're taking the time to be still.

1. The first is that you can have a lot of internal dialogue and inner turbulence. So when you sit down, you actually experience a lot of thoughts and activity inside. This experience is okay and natural. You are experiencing the momentum of the mind over many years of activity. You have been <u>doing</u> too much, and when you decide to take the time to *be*, the doing still goes on inside, because you've been doing so much for so many years. The point is to sit through this as it is the nervous system's way of actually dumping and releasing stress, and that's perfectly okay.

2. The second thing that can happen is that we can fall asleep, and that's okay, as well, because that's just the nervous system catching up on sleep. If this continues each day, it is feedback that you need to gain more hours of sleep before midnight so you can wake up fully rested.

3. The third thing that can happen is that we have an experience of complete stillness and enter into what Primordial Sound Meditation calls "the gap." That's great, too, as this is quite fulfilling and enjoyable.

The point is not to judge the experience, but just to observe the experience and accept the experience as it is. With meditation, there is no goal, no striving, nothing to accomplish, which is all found in the mind. It is to just switch off the mind and let go. Here is how ...

The Practice

The first thing is to choose an environment where you can sit undisturbed. You want to make sure that you can come to this place every day to take the time to be still. Having a place at home that you can dedicate yourself to supports you in keeping it consistent as it creates a positive anchor that triggers your positive feelings around sitting still.

With meditation, there is no goal, no striving, nothing to accomplish, which is all found in the mind. It is to just switch off the mind and let go.

Make sure you have a chair or sofa where you can sit

with a straight back. When preparing the environment, shut the door; if it is dark, opt for candlelight, instead of bright lights. Sit in an upright position with a straight back and your hands on your lap facing upward.

Take three deep breaths in through your nose and exhale out through your nose. Breathe into your belly, which should be moving out when you breathe in. On the out breath, restrict the air at the back of your throat, slowing down the out breath through your nose. This is called pranayama breathing, or belly breathing and with these three deep breaths, we're actually able to release a lot of stress and still the mind very rapidly.

Then focus on your breathing. Breathe normally in and out through the nose. Any time you get caught up in your thoughts, either the past or the future, become aware of that. The awareness that is who you are becomes aware of that and then comes back to focus on the breath—the reason being that when you're focusing on your breath, you are not thinking—you're getting out of your own way, and you're being here and now.

Sit for 20 minutes or more to gain maximum benefit from this exercise. If you've never done it before, start with five minutes and build up to 20 minutes over a couple of weeks. Ideally, do this in the morning, as the sun rises, and in the evening, as the sun sets, before you eat.

Practicing Acceptance

Judgment is one of the root causes of excessive mental activity. The mind loves to judge situations, circumstances, and people. In psychology, this is called projection, which is the unconscious transfer of our thoughts and emotions onto another person. Due to the mind's inability to accept or tolerate difference in others or the situation, we "judge" it and wish it to be another way. Typically, this is accompanied by specific emotions, which are experienced at different degrees of strength. Anytime we are judging or someone pushes one of our buttons and we are triggered emotionally, then we know we are projecting. This means it is not about the other person; it is not about the situation or even the circumstance. It is about you and what is going on inside you. The outside situation is triggering a judgement and emotions because you cannot accept them as they are. For those of us who are trapped in this, we are constantly being pushed

The past is gone, don't mind, the future is uncertain, don't mind, the now is as it is, pay attention.

and pulled around by outer circumstances. We blame those

circumstances for how we feel and the results we get. We struggle against reality as it is and suffer because of this. This mental and emotional rollercoaster ride takes up a lot of time and energy. We are caught in our heads, projecting it onto others and the world we live in. This creates and reinforces mental activity, leading to inner turbulence, stress, and disharmony, which leads to dis-ease.

How do we free ourselves from this and take back our power? Accept everything as it is, not as you wish it to be. Each moment is as it is.

Stop "Minding" or doing mind. Each time you catch yourself not being able to accept the moment, STOP! Focus on your breathing and breathe deeply from your belly, in through your nose and out through your nose. Breathe through the emotions, feel them and keep breathing until they subside. Say to yourself, *"It is as it is, let it go!"* This is not to say that you don't do anything about the current situation—from this place of acceptance, you then are able

Acceptance is a very powerful tool that helps us to be present and stay rooted in the now, as does the practice of meditation.

to respond creatively, instead of reacting.

You are free from your external situation; it can no longer trigger a predictable reaction in you. You are still, present, silent, and in your power. From this place, you are then able to respond creatively in the appropriate manner to achieve your desired outcome. This is freedom, this is empowerment, and this is right action.

Acceptance is a very powerful tool that helps us to be present and stay rooted firmly in the now, as does the practice of meditation.

Listening

The third method I would like to share with you is the practice and art of listening.

Listening is one of the simplest and most basic ways to enter into the now. Listening means being present; it means to forget yourself completely, to enter into the other person's world. It is being present, forgetting yourself, being attentive to the other and genuinely caring about them, being passive, observing them without any internal dialogue to think about a comeback or construct an answer. This is being present; this is being with another fully. If you cannot forget about yourself and focus on another fully and completely, you can never listen.

You can fake listening, you can pretend you are

listening, you can say yes or no, smile and respond, but you are not there—you are somewhere else other than with that person. Of course, they feel that. They feel you are not there with them. The greatest need for a human being is to be heard, met, and understood. If you can't forget yourself and truly BE with another, you will never be able to fulfil that person's needs, and you will never be able to attain high-end trust with them. When you listen, you have to become passive and receptive, become the feminine, open. Put away the masculine problem solver who wants to cut through obstacles and fix it. Sit, focus on the other, be attentive, observe, listen with the heart to understand, really understand the other, be passive and open and watch what happens to how people respond to you. Watch what happens to your relationships when you relate this way with others.

The greatest need for a human being is to be heard, met, and understood.

Even when you are not with others and you are on your own, you can practice listening. Just listen, become aware of the sounds around you, observe what is happening, take it all in, and BE HERE NOW. It is from this moment that all greatness is created, it this moment that is the source of all inspiration, and it is this moment that opens the door to your success.

These are three very powerful techniques that you can use on a day-to-day basis that will support you in losing your mind and coming to your senses. You will have a more meaningful life, and the more meaning that your life is full of, the better you will perform and the better your quality of life will be. The more you are able to apply these methods, the more successful you will become, because success is not measured through acquiring things or through the amount of money that you earn. Your level of success is determined by how happy and fulfilled you are, and that is determined by how much you can live in the now.

Remember that this is something anyone can do to improve their life, its meaning, and their performance. We're all human beings. We all have an ego. We all have a conscious, unconscious, and super conscious mind, for example. We all are born; we all die. Most of us have two arms, two legs and a heart. That's the human condition.

These teachings are not something new; they have been taught for millennia and has been mastered by the sages of the old cultures. These teachings are starting to be remembered and revived in this modern-day existence. Many in the business and sporting world practice and rely on them for top performance. The East has been practicing them for centuries—learning how to master the mind and transcend it and get out of the way. The West has been learning about how to create wealth and material success through doing, doing, doing. The East has learned about being. But now the two are starting to become integrated, and the West is starting to learn about the East, and the East is starting to learn about the West. We're starting to become more whole as a race, and that is a great thing.

The results that come from putting these methods into practice are multi-fold. For example, working with world-class leaders in Fortune 500 companies, the very first method I teach them to increase their performance is meditation, giving them the exact techniques that we mentioned earlier, which they put into practice. They kept a journal. They were committed to taking the time to just "be" on a daily basis, and they started to notice that they were able to make better decisions, they started to calm down, and they were reacting less. They were able to respond more creatively. Their relationships started to change with their peers. They had more energy. They started to perform better and got better performance reviews. They felt more fulfilled and happier ... many benefits just from practicing one method. The same with athletes, they also noticed that their performance went up, that they were able to tap into that zone more easily and experience it more often. These are some of the benefits people start to experience relatively quickly once they learn how to get out of the way of themselves, lose their mind, and come to their senses.

It's always a choice; you have a choice in everything you do. What will the consequences be if you don't put these methods to the test? The mind is very strong, and the more the mind is in control, the more its conditioning will start to affect the type of results you create. You must, if you want to fulfil your full potential in your life, learn how you work as a human being. That's why I'm recommending in this book that you work on two fronts. Work on mastering the mind and the emotions and its programming, and get rid of that old programming and replace it with new supportive, resourceful programing. At the same time, learn to transcend the mind and go to that place where top athletes or people go when they're self-actualized and have peak experiences. Learn to go to that

> You must, if you want to fulfil our full potential in life, know how you work as a human being.

place where you can feel so fulfilled because you are so present, so here, right here, right now, that you have a "no mind" experience and perform literally out of your mind. It's your choice, and it is in your hands.

"To the mind that is still,
the whole universe surrenders."

~ Lao Tzu

5.

PRESENCE EQUALS PERFORMANCE

"The more I am in the here and now, the more I have access to who I am—infinite possibilities."

~ Timothy Carroll

PRESENCE IS YOUR most natural state. It is who you are when you are born, and the present moment is always here following you wherever you go. We cannot not be in the present moment as the present moment is all we have. Presence is all that matters, all that counts, and in truth all there is. This moment right here and right now is the present as I write these words. As you read them right now, that is also the present. You cannot escape it; it is always here and always will be. It is who you are.

The question is, at what degree are you experiencing this moment, this now? Even while reading these words, you can be thinking about something else. You can be in the future, thinking about what might be or what you want to achieve tomorrow. You can also be thinking about the past, what happened, why it

> **Presence is all that matters, all that counts, and in truth, all there is.**

happened, or great things that you experienced.

This all occurs in your mind. The past and the future are all a construct of the mind, and the present, well, that is right here and now—it is what you are observing, feeling, and hearing right now.

In summary, there are only three experiences you can have at a mental level. You can be in the past re-member-ing, (reattaching yourself to something that is gone) you can be in the future imagin-ing (constructing an image of something that has not happened), or you can be here in the present, observ-ing (seeing things as they are without judgment). This chapter is focused on being present and how this supports top performance.

When you are present, you are experiencing your own presence. Being present is a gift to yourself, and when you give yourself this gift, it supports your happiness, fulfilment, and ability to achieve your full potential in life. As Abraham Maslow attested to, they are self-actualized people. They are people who are fulfilling their potential. Why? Because your

> **The past is history, the future is a mystery, and the now is a gift; that is why they call it the present.**

potential, your full potential, is found in the present moment. It's not found in your thoughts. It's not found in the future. It's not found in the past. It's not found in things. It's found in a state of being which can only be experienced by being here now. And it just so happens that peak performance occurs in this same space. Whether you are a mum or dad, a top leader or world-class athlete, peak performance is all achieved through accessing this magical place called the present moment.

> **Your potential, your full potential, is found in the present moment.**

Learning from the Best

Having been a New Zealand Representative in barefoot water-skiing, I think there is a lot to learn from athletes about being in the present moment. Top athletes are great examples, because in the midst of dynamic action, athletes have tapped into the present moment. They become so externally focused on what they are doing they have entered into the gap between their thoughts. They have dived fully into the now.

The great Brazilian football player Pelé described this as "effortless play," that he had an experience of time slowing down, that he was able to run past the players effortlessly, it was as if they were standing still, and before he knew it, it was a goal. He describes his experience as easy, effortless, and free. When you actually play that in real time, everything was happening in such a dynamic action, it was an amazing performance. But for him, he had a transcendental experience. He transcended his mind and operated at a completely different operational level, which allowed him to perform that way.

Top athletes are able to do this consciously: tap into this place of what we call "the zone" or this place called "the flow," as Mihaly Csikszentmihalyi talks about in his book, *The Flow*. We can learn a lot about how to do this from these people who have experienced this.

In seeking a great example of a world-class athlete who I know and would say has really mastered this, I refer back to William Trubridge, the current world record holder and world champion free diver, who has, in the purest form of free diving Constant Weight No Fins (CNF), dived to 101 meters and returned to the surface on one breath. To do this, he has to go to a completely different operational level mentally, which supports him to go to a different level physically. To do this, he transcends his mind and all of his emotions that come with it.

As I mentioned earlier in this book, he uses his breath, he ignores his thoughts, and he dives into the silence between them and enters into an experience he describes as becoming one with the ocean, so that there's no boundary between his body and the ocean. He *becomes* the ocean. And it's only through that experience that he's able to transcend fear, transcend any negative beliefs, and his body starts operating at a higher level.

As he descends, he relaxes more and more. His body adjusts to not breathing by conserving oxygen and slowing his heart rate down to less than 30 beats a minute. Through training his body to operate on low levels of oxygen, he is able to hold his breath for over 7 minutes while just being still and for 4 to 5 minutes when diving actively. He has trained his body and mind to do things that no human being has been able to do before, and it is all possible because he is able to let go of fear, the past, and the future, and be here and now. With a lot of training, both physically and mentally, William has managed to master himself and be able to tap into that present moment at will, and stay there. That's the tough part while diving; the body is prepared, but the tough part is to stay present each time he dives and ignore what's going on in his mind and the emotions that distract him from diving deep into his own self and into the deep ocean.

Traps of the Mind

We are going to address the three biggest mistakes that people make that prevent them from accessing the present moment and top performance.

Attachment to the Result

People have goals and desires, and they become deeply attached to that result and attaining it. The mind becomes so attached that it creates a stress response, and their thoughts and emotions start to run the game, creating an internal turbulence. People tend to work harder, push themselves longer hours, and get out of balance even more. Just like the 100m runner who is coming to the end of her race, it is important to let go, relax, and hold onto your form to increase speed or to accelerate yourself across the line. The same goes for people attaining their goals, whether it is in business or sport. To achieve what you want, you must learn to let go of the attachment to it and relax into it. Continue to take action, continue to stay focused on what you want, see it in your mind's eye, but let go of the rest.

> Life is a paradox; to create what you want, you must let go.

When I say the rest, I mean the internal stories and stress that come with desiring something too much. Life is a paradox; to create what you want, you must let go.

Procrastination or Preparation

Repetition is the mother of all learning. I found that to be able to let go as an athlete and come fully into the moment, I needed to be prepared fully for the coming event or the performance. If I was not fully prepared, I could not trust myself to do what I had been training to do; the nerves would kick in and tension and anxiety would increase, affecting performance.

Preparation requires you to be proactive. Proactivity is to act in advance and set yourself up for success, as opposed to being reactive and leaving it to the last minute. To be able to be proactive requires you to be responsible— to take responsibility for what needs to be done to attain your goals and then act. This is a sign of maturity and that you are independent and mature enough to decide what you want, know what to do to achieve it, then act upon that in advance.

To be prepared also requires you to be good at following procedures and to act upon a plan, system, and routines that you set up for yourself to create success. The opposite is to keep your options open, not making decisions about what you will act on today to get to where you want to be, and creating systems for success but you have problems following them.

These two mental programs I am addressing are hard wired into our neurology. The first one I addressed is called Level of Activity, which reflects our ability to act and the speed of action. The second one is Planning Style, which determines how we act or do things in a certain way.

The preferred ways of thinking and acting for success to become prepared are Proactive and Procedural. To discover these in yourself or employees can be done through observing their behaviour or through "The Identity Compass," a state-of-the-art profiling system measuring preferred thinking preferences in the context of career and sport.

The ironic side to this is that specific ways of thinking determine ways of acting in the world, which supports you to be present when needed so you can relax and let go due to good preparation.

The following is a description of a specific thinking preference called Level of Activity from an Identity Compass Report. It looks at how active the person is when given a task. Are they proactive or do they procrastinate and consequently become reactive?

Level of Activity – This thinking structure has to do with the speed of action or reaction. If your results are balanced (difference at 10% maximum) between Pre-Active and Re-Active on a high level (over 60%), you are regarded as Active. At a low level (below 50%), you are regarded as Non-Reactive.

The diagram below shows this person has a preferred thinking preference that is Active. From this, we can then predict how she will behave. See below for the Active description.

Based on the answers you have given, it shows that you are using:

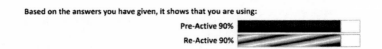

Pre-Active 90%
Re-Active 90%

Pre-Active: This preference causes a person to act in a preventative way, not knowing whether the subject of the reaction will happen or not. For example, if a report has to be written with a due date in four weeks, this person would start immediately. He/she acts in advance and in time. The preference reflects prevention.

Active: A person with this thinking preference would start to prepare the report after maybe two weeks' time. Changes are dealt with at once and spontaneously. This thinking preference is important for short reaction times.

Re-Active: A person with this thinking preference would

begin to write during the last two or three days. Changes are dealt with only after thorough reflection. This preference is useful in quality control jobs.

Non-Reactive: A person with this preference does not change his/her pace due to outer influences. He/she is somehow stubborn. She would write the report at the last day or not at all. He/she can sit on things. This preference has its merits when it comes to getting things done while dealing with many obstacles.

Distractions

The third thing that prevents us from being in the present moment is distractions.

Distractions come in many shapes and sizes, from all around us. They move us into our head and thinking, into the future, into the past, and prevent us from being fully here now.

The more present you are, the greater you will perform.

Some of the typical distractions I have found are:

- Too many tasks at one time.
- Screens like the TV, iPad, phone and computer.
- Interruptions, such as emails or phone calls.

- Our thoughts stopping us from being focused on the task at hand.

This chapter is called Presence Equals Performance – the more present you are, the greater you will perform. If you haven't learned how to do that, then your performance is going to be inconsistent. It doesn't matter whether you're an athlete or whether you're a business leader, being present is going to support you in being able to creatively respond to situations, circumstances, and people, stay focused and act consistently.

The business world is starting to really wake up to the fact that they've got to learn techniques around how to work with their staff's conditioning and their thinking programs so they can develop and improve their behaviours and results. They have got to learn how to manage stress levels in their staff. They've got to learn how to support leadership and their people in being present and performing to their best. This is transformational leadership, and this is how to work with the human capital of a company to grow and improve its results in a sustainable way.

Every day, I work with leaders who are very aware of this and want to really learn how to lead through being present, through being an example of what is possible, through inspiring others through their example. Great leaders have this presence about them; people with presence who lead are better performers. This cascades down through the business, because leadership is all about being a role model, which is the most successful character trait of a leader. You become whom you associate with. So, as a leader, you're going to affect the people around you; and if you're present, those people are going to very much know that you are present with them and will feel understood and respected. You'll be able to respond more creatively to those people and their needs. Trust will be deeply established as the leader shows up consistently every day and does not have a Jekyll and Hyde personality.

Evolutionary leadership is very much about being present, and modern day leaders are finally waking up to the power of presence in performance.

> **Evolutionary leadership is very much about being present.**

The Challenge

The big challenge with being present is that the majority of people are unconscious and unaware of what being present is and how to do it. They don't know the power of the mind and that they are at its mercy. They are constantly doing to try and achieve what they want, pushing themselves and their results. The person who is able to tap into the present is a person who is performing to their full potential. However we've learned the opposite. We've learned that to act, to do, and to take massive action and do, do, do is what's required to achieve.

There's an old Zen saying, *"Chop wood, carry water."* What that means is that while we're chopping wood and carrying water and doing that activity, we can be very present, very here, right now. That's the key: in the midst of dynamic activity, how can we be so externally focused, how can we be so present that it's effortless? So the principle of doing less and achieving more is the principle that businesses, athletes, and people the world over want to master, because it's from that place that we can achieve our potential and perform to our fullest. Activity is achieved effortlessly while in the present moment, with no mind involved.

The spinoff is that there are many other benefits that come with being present in life. Health wise, there are enormous benefits. We know that those people who meditate on a regular basis have a far less chance of getting cancer, far less chance of getting a mental illness—they are much healthier and actually live

We feel more fulfilled and happy when we're tapped into the now.

longer. So just the pure health benefits are phenomenal. As a parent, husband, or wife, it's amazing how it affects and develops relationships. We become closer to the people around us. We're able to relate better with people. We feel more fulfilled and happy when we're tapped into the now.

The actual character traits of self-actualized people who are very present, who have all of their human needs fulfilled and are exploding out of the top of Maslow's Hierarchy of Needs, show that they're very happy people. They have peak experiences often. They experience bliss. They experience a lot of love. They contribute a lot to society. They do what they love. They're not concerned about making money; they are focused on contribution. The ultimate benefit is that being present supports you in naturally fulfilling your potential as a human being or self-actualizing, as Maslow described it.

Maslow's Characteristics of Self-Actualizers

- *Efficient perceptions of reality.* Self-actualizers are able to judge situations correctly and honestly. They are very sensitive to the fake and dishonest, and are free to see reality 'as it is.'

- *Comfortable acceptance of self, others and nature.* Self-actualizers accept their own human nature with all its flaws. The shortcomings of others and the contradictions of the human condition are accepted with humor and tolerance.

- *Reliant on own experiences and judgement.* Independent, not reliant on culture and environment to form opinions and views.

- *Spontaneous and natural.* True to oneself, rather than being how others want.

- *Task centering.* Most of Maslow's subjects had a mission to fulfil in life or some task or problem 'beyond' themselves (instead of outside of themselves) to pursue. Humanitarians such as Albert Schweitzer are considered to have possessed this quality.

- *Autonomy.* Self-actualizers are free from reliance on external authorities or other people. They tend to be resourceful and independent.

- *Continued freshness of appreciation.* The self-actualizer seems to constantly renew appreciation of life's basic goods. A sunset or a flower will be experienced as intensely time after time as it was at first. There is an "innocence of vision," like that of an artist or child.

- *Profound interpersonal relationships.* The interpersonal relationships of self-actualizers are marked by deep loving bonds.

- *Comfort with solitude.* Despite their satisfying relationships with others, self-actualizing people value solitude and are comfortable being alone.

- *Non-hostile sense of humor.* This refers to the ability to laugh at oneself.

- *Peak experiences.* All of Maslow's subjects reported the frequent occurrence of peak experiences (temporary moments of self-actualization). These occasions were marked by feelings of ecstasy, harmony, and deep meaning. Self-actualizers reported feeling at one with the universe, stronger and calmer than ever before, filled with light, beauty, goodness, and so forth.

- *Socially compassionate.* Possessing humanity.

- *Few friends.* Few close intimate friends, rather than many superficial relationships.

The above is from Wikipedia https://en.**wikipedia**.org/

Role Models

There are some unique people in the world who are role models of being present and are even considered to be self-actualizers. I would like to lift up some of these people, so you can look further into what is possible and perhaps learn from them.

Nelson Rolihlahla Mandela (/mæn'dɛlə/; 18 July 1918 – 5 December 2013) was a South African anti-apartheid revolutionary, politician, and philanthropist, who served as President of South Africa from 1994 to 1999. He was the country's first black chief executive, and the first elected in a fully representative democratic election. His government focused on dismantling the legacy of apartheid through tackling institutionalised racism and fostering racial reconciliation. Politically a African nationalist and democratic socialist, he served as President of the African National Congress (ANC) party from 1991 to 1997.

Mandela served 27 years in prison, initially on Robben Island, and later in Pollsmoor Prison and Victor Verster Prison. An international campaign lobbied for his release, which was granted in 1990 amid escalating civil strife. Mandela joined negotiations with President F. W. de Klerk to abolish apartheid and establish multiracial elections in 1994, in which he led the ANC to victory and became South Africa's first black president. He published his autobiography in 1995. Leading South Africa's Government of National Unity, which promulgated a new constitution,

Mandela also created the Truth and Reconciliation Commission to investigate past human rights abuses.

Declining a second presidential term, he was succeeded by his deputy, Thabo Mbeki. Mandela became an elder statesman, focusing on charitable work in combating poverty and HIV/AIDS through the Nelson Mandela Foundation.

Mandela was a controversial figure for much of his life. Denounced as a communist terrorist by critics, he faced particular opposition from supporters of apartheid. Conversely, he gained international acclaim for his activism, having received more than 250 honours, including the 1993 Nobel Peace Prize, the US Presidential Medal of Freedom, and the Soviet Lenin Peace Prize. He is held in deep respect within South Africa, where he is often referred to by his Xhosa clan name, **Madiba**, or as **Tata** ("Father"), and described as the "Father of the Nation."

Mohandas Karamchand Gandhi (/ˈɡɑːndi,_Hindustani; 2 October 1869 – 30 January 1948) was the preeminent leader of the Indian independence movement in British-ruled India. Employing nonviolent civil disobedience, Gandhi led India to independence and inspired movements for civil rights and freedom across the world.

The honorific **Mahatma** (Sanskrit: high-souled, vener-able), applied to him first in 1914 in South Africa, is now used worldwide. He is also called **Bapu** (Gujarati: endear-ment for "father," "papa") in India. In common parlance in India, he is often called **Gandhiji**. He is unofficially called the Father of the Nation.

Gandhi famously led Indians in challenging the British-imposed salt tax with the 400 km (250 mi) Dandi Salt March in 1930, and later in calling for the British to *Quit India* in 1942. He was imprisoned for many years, upon many occasions, in both South Africa and India. Gandhi attempted to practise nonviolence and truth in all situations, and advocated that others do the same. He lived modestly in a self-sufficient residential community and wore the traditional Indian *dhoti* and shawl, woven with yarn hand-spun on a *charkha*. He ate simple vegetarian food, and also undertook long fasts as a means of both self-purification and social protest.

Gandhi's vision of an independent India based on religious pluralism, however, was challenged in the early 1940s by a new Muslim nationalism which was demanding a separate Muslim homeland carved out of India. Eventually, in August 1947, Britain granted independence, but the

British Indian Empire was partitioned into two dominions, a Hindu-majority India and Muslim Pakistan.

Nathuram Godse, a Hindu nationalist, assassinated Gandhi on 30 January 1948 by firing three bullets into his chest at point-blank range.

His birthday, 2 October, is commemorated as Gandhi Jayanti, a national holiday, and worldwide as the International Day of Nonviolence.

Martin Luther King, Jr. (January 15, 1929 – April 4, 1968) was an American Baptist minister, activist, humanitarian, and leader in the African-American Civil Rights Movement. He is best known for his role in the advancement of civil rights, using nonviolent civil disobedience based on his Christian beliefs.

King became a civil rights activist early in his career. He led the 1955 Montgomery Bus Boycott and helped found the Southern Christian Leadership Conference (SCLC) in 1957, serving as its first president. With the SCLC, King led an unsuccessful 1962 struggle against segregation in Albany, Georgia (the Albany Movement), and helped organize the 1963 nonviolent protests in Birmingham, Alabama. King also helped to organize the 1963 March on Washington, where he delivered his famous "I Have a Dream" speech.

There, he established his reputation as one of the greatest orators in American history.

On October 14, 1964, King received the Nobel Peace Prize for combating racial inequality through nonviolence. In 1965, he helped to organize the Selma to Montgomery marches, and the following year he and SCLC took the movement north to Chicago to work on segregated housing. In the final years of his life, King expanded his focus to include poverty and speak against the Vietnam War, alienating many of his liberal allies with a 1967 speech titled "Beyond Vietnam."

In 1968, King was planning a national occupation of Washington, D.C., to be called the Poor People's Campaign, when he was assassinated on April 4 in Memphis, Tennessee. His death was followed by riots in many U.S. cities.

King was posthumously awarded the Presidential Medal of Freedom and the Congressional Gold Medal. Martin Luther King, Jr. Day was established as a holiday in numerous cities and states beginning in 1971, and as a U.S. federal holiday in 1986. Hundreds of streets in the U.S. have been renamed in his honor, and a county in Washington State was also renamed for him. The Martin Luther King, Jr.

Memorial on the National Mall in Washington, D.C., was dedicated in 2011.

Thích Nhất Hạnh, born as Nguyen Xuan Bao on October 11, 1926), is a Vietnamese Zen Buddhist monk, teacher, author, poet and peace activist. He lives in the Plum Village Monastery in the Dordogne region in the South of France travelling internationally to give retreats and talks. He coined the term Engaged Buddhism in his book, *Vietnam: Lotus in a Sea of Fire.* A long-term exile, he was given permission to make his first return trip to Vietnam in 2005.

Nhất Hạnh has published more than 100 books, including more than 40 in English. Nhat Hanh is active in the peace movement, promoting non-violent solutions to conflict and he also refrains from animal product consumption as a means of non-violence toward non-human animals.

Eckhart Tolle, born **Ulrich Leonard Tölle** on February 16, 1948), is a German-born resident of Canada, best known as the author of *The Power of Now* and *A New Earth.* In 2011, he was listed by the Watkins Review as the most spiritually influential person in the world. In 2008, a *New York Times* writer called Tolle "the most popular spiritual author in the United States."

Tolle has said that he was depressed for much of his life until he underwent, at age 29, an "inner transformation." He then spent several years wandering and unemployed "in a state of deep bliss" before becoming a spiritual teacher. Later, he moved to North America, where he began writing his first book, *The Power of Now*, which was published in 1997 and reached the *New York Times* Best Seller lists in 2000.

The Power of Now and *A New Earth* sold an estimated three million and five million copies respectively in North America by 2009. In 2008, approximately 35 million people participated in a series of 10 live webinars with Tolle and television talk show host Oprah Winfrey. Tolle is not identified with any particular religion, but he has been influenced by a wide range of spiritual works. He has lived in Vancouver, Canada since 1995.

The above is from Wikipedia https://en.**wikipedia**.org/

The key to top performance and fulfilment is to learn to be present in every moment. And that *is* also the challenge. This is what these roles models that I highlighted above made a priority in their lives. We all need role models to look up to, learn from, and gain support from. The practice of meditation daily is one tool, if not the tool, that will help you get there. The meditation we practice carries into every moment in our lives, supporting us to be more productive, happy, healthy, and stress free. To be present with our colleagues, or in the midst of a crisis. To be present when we're making love or with our life partner, and to be present with ourselves; this is the ultimate gift that we can give to the world. Make it your goal and see what happens to the quality of your life.

> **To be present with ourselves is the ultimate gift that we can give to the world.**

Self-Enquiry

In my experience, along with the practice of meditation, self-enquiry has been the most powerful tool in supporting me to stay present. I learned about self-enquiry from a man who is no longer with us, a man from India called Ramana.

Ramana Maharshi (30 December 1879 – 14 April 1950) was an Indian yogi. He was born Venkataraman Iyer, in Tiruchuli, Tamil Nadu, South India, and given the name Bhagavan Sri Ramana Maharshi in 1907 by one of his first devotees, Ganapati Muni. This would be the name by which he became more widely known.

Venkataraman was said to have permanently lost his sense of individual selfhood in 1896, at the age of 16, an event that he later described as enlightenment. Six weeks later, he left his family home in Madurai and journeyed to the holy mountain Arunachala, in Tiruvannamalai, where he would remain for the rest of his life.

Although his first years in Tiruvannamalai were spent in solitude, he soon attracted devotees, and in later years, a community grew up around him, where he was available 24 hours a day. Although worshipped by thousands, he never received private gifts and treated all with equal respect. Since the 1930s, his teachings have been popularised in the west.

Throughout the years, Ramana Maharshi responded to many questions on spiritual matters, but always insisted that silence was the purest teaching. In response to questions on self-liberation and the classic texts on yoga and Vedanta, Ramana recommended self-enquiry as the principal way to awaken to the "I-I," realise the self and attain liberation. He also recommended Bhakti, as well as giving his approval to a variety of paths and practices.

The above is from Wikipedia https://en.**wikipedia**.org/

When he was a young man, his story goes that he had an overwhelming fear of death. And so he lay down on the dirt floor in his house and said, *"If I'm going to die, I'm going to die right now."* And death came and took him, but not physically.

Mentally, he had a peak experience where his mind stopped, and he merged with the All That Is, Was, and Ever Will Be. From that point on, he sat in silence for 25 years, and people would come into his presence and their mind would stop. This man is an example of someone who transcended the mind and entered into the now and the gap between our thoughts and established himself there. Many others have attained this state of consciousness whom we know as enlightened Masters.

Ramana's recommendation was to practice self-enquiry. How do you still the mind and be able to reside in the present without leaving it? He asked people to start to enquire by asking themselves the question, *"Who am I?* To actually enquire into the existence of self. This self-enquiry is to enquire into the source of everything and every action—to turn the mind back on itself and realize the source of who you really are. Who is it that's sitting here? Who is it that's breathing? Who is it that's walking down the street? Through self-enquiry, you can really learn to be present in every moment.

I found this was extremely powerful in my own sport and life—to use self-enquiry to still my mind and tap into this present moment. I can recall a time when I was on the dock before performing in a water-skiing competition and I asked myself the question, "Who am I?" My mind became very still, all anxiety dropped away and I found myself here and now. If I noticed any activity in my mind again or anxiety about competing or failing, I'd ask, "Who's competing today?" "Who fails?" and my mind would stop. What was left was silence, presence, this moment here and now. I used this as a tool to tap into who I was, which is the force that resides between my thoughts—my full potential.

In my experience, the number one thing you can do to stay present in every moment, is to practice self-enquiry on a regular basis. To not allow the power of the mind to take over who you are, which is the now, this moment. You are that! My challenge to you is to apply this chapter to your life and track the benefits. Notice what it does for you and the results that you get over the days and weeks to come.

> **Through self-enquiry, you can really learn to be present in every moment.**

"When you reach that elite level, 90 percent is mental and 10 percent is physical. You are against yourself, not against the other athlete."

**~ Dick Fosbury,
High Jump Olympic Champion
and World Record Holder**

IT'S TIME TO EVOLVE

EVOLUTIONARY LEADERS are revolutionary by nature. They like to create paradigm shifts, challenge the status quo, and leave a legacy. These type of leaders as self-aware, emotionally intelligent, people orientated, top-end performers. They lead by example and are role models for those who lead. They are addicted to the process of getting better. They lead from a higher purpose and vision, fuelled by making a difference and developing better people, leadership, and results for all concerned.

Evolutionary leaders have a few traits in common that I will share below.

They are transformational. They transform themselves, their people, and the organization to obtain better results through doing less and achieving more. They work on the business and the people to explode business performance. They have a clear vision and work towards this by empowering people and helping them to achieve their potential.

They create collaboration. Developing relationships between all stakeholders requires win-win thinking and behaviours, developing highly independent and inter-dependent people. They know that silo thinking does not work, and they encourage collaboration between people and business' units to achieve the goals.

They keep their ego checked. Focusing on being the change that they want to see in the world, they act as role models. They know that they are neither above nor below others. They have confidence and high self-esteem. They value themselves and others, creating trust and strong relationships.

They have integrity. They are transparent, open and vulnerable, genuine and authentic. They are not moved by what other people think about them. They know when they're doing a good job and know that it's okay to make mistakes. They are 100% committed to the growth and evolution of themselves and the larger whole.

They are super present. They have the ability to listen deeply and proactively. They are dedicated to connecting with their source through the practice of meditation or mindfulness. They are calm and centred. They ask great questions and empower people to find the answers within.

My hope is that through reading this book you are inspired to develop yourself and your desire to be an Evolutionary Leader. One who is committed to the evolutionary values and behaviours that will transform the results you get at home, in the office, in your community, and on our planet. The way leadership and the people who follow them relate to the planet and all that exists upon her must change. The way we are living on this planet is not sustainable, we are killing our home, which we only have one of, threatening the existence of the human race. In this critical time, we need to evolve how we think about others and the world at large, how we treat the environment and the nature on it, and how we will act now for our children and our children's children. To achieve this, a shift in consciousness is required, and that means you. If not, then who? It's time to evolve—will you?

The way leadership and the people who follow them relate to the planet and all that exists upon her must change.

ABOUT THE AUTHOR

TIMOTHY IS A recognized expert in organizational and behavioural change. He has consulted and delivered strategic interventions to national and multi-national companies and their leadership around the world, supporting them in creating lasting results for nearly two decades.

Prior to founding the Carroll Consultancy Group, Timothy worked for and studied with numerous world leaders in the field of human development, self-actualizing psychology, and cognitive behavioural sciences. His philosophy is that he never stops learning, and he has continually sought out the best in the world to learn from, as he did in his career as an elite athlete.

Timothy has represented New Zealand in Barefoot Water-skiing at 4 World Championships, first being picked for his country at just 16 years of age. He regularly performed to his best in the big tournaments, placing 19th overall and making the finals (top 12) in the jump event in his first ever world championships in Melbourne, Australia.

Timothy has also worked with many successful individuals in the field of business and sport, such as professional footballers, golfers, and ice hockey players to name a few. In 2008, he attended the Beijing Olympics as a performance coach.

Timothy's genuineness, experience, passion for growth, and "Down Under" personality make him a natural and comfortable person to work with who supports his clients in creating outstanding long-term results. Timothy currently resides with his family in the Bahamas.

INTERVIEWS

SPECIAL THANKS GOES out to William Trubridge for taking the time to share his thoughts on peak performance and how he gets to the depths that he does on a single breath.

To Matt Wallden for sharing his knowledge and time re the secrets of health and their effect on our physiology and performance.

To the countless people over the course of my life that I have interviewed, taken to lunch, and been influenced by. All the learning that I have received and put into practice is between these pages.

MEDITATORS

HERE IS A list of some celebrities that have learnt to meditate and have been practicing on a regular basis.

Phil Jackson

Clint Eastwood

Michael Jordan

Leonardo Di Caprio

LeBron James

Tina Turner

Orlando Blom

Richard Gere

The Beatles

Katy Perry

Hugh Jackman

Naomi Watts

Howard Stern

Heather Graham

Ellen DeGeneres

Jennifer Aniston

Kristen Bell

Nicole Kidman

Jim Carrey

Jerry Seinfeld

Will Smith

50 Cents

Oprah Winfrey

Steven Seagal

Russell Brand

Sting

Ray Dalio

Cameron Diaz

Sheryl Crow

Liv Tyler

Martin Scorsese

Deepak Chopra

Jeff Bridges

Madonna

Dax Shepard

Eva Mendes

Lady Gaga

Goldie Hawn

Susan Sarandon

Paula Abdul

Shirley MacLaine

Mick Jagger

Moby

Dr. Oz

David Lynch

Bill Ford

Arianna Huffington

Derek Jeter

Chicago Bulls with Phil Jackson

Jane Fonda

Rosie O'Donnell

Steve Jobs

George Lucas

Lenny Kravitz

Joe Namath

Ben Foster

Kobe Bryant

Russell Simmons

Larry Brilliant

Barry Zito

LA Lakers with Phil Jackson

Seattle Hawks with Pete Carroll

ENVIRONMENTAL CAUSE

MAUI'S DOLPHIN OR *popoto* (*Cephalorhynchus hectori maui*) is the world's rarest and smallest known subspecies of dolphin.

They are a subspecies of the Hector's dolphin. Maui's dolphins are only found off the west coast of New Zealand's North Island. Hector's and Maui's are New Zealand's only endemic cetaceans. Maui's dolphins are generally found close to shore in groups or pods of several dolphins. They are generally seen in water shallower than 20 m, but may also range further offshore.

The dolphin is threatened by set-netting and trawling. Based on estimates from 2012, in May 2014, the World Wildlife Fund in New Zealand launched "The Last 55" campaign, calling for a full ban over what it believed is their entire range. The International Whaling Commission supports more fishing restrictions, but the New Zealand government has resisted the demands and questioned the reliability of the evidence presented to the IWC that Maui's dolphins inhabit the areas they are said to inhabit. In June 2014, the government decided to open up 3000 km^2 of the West Coast North Island Marine Mammal Sanctuary – the main habitat of the Maui's dolphin – for oil drilling. This amounts to one-quarter of the total sanctuary area. In May 2015, estimates suggested that the population had declined to 43-47 individuals, of which only 10 were mature females.

The above is from Wikipedia https://en.**wikipedia**.org/

Please support the smallest and rarest dolphin in the world.
http://www.wwf.org.nz/maui_dolphin/

Join Hector's and Maui's Dolphins SOS on Facebook
or visit www.hectorsdolphins.com

BOOKS

Phil Jackson, *Eleven Rings*

James Kerr, *Legacy*

Paul Chek, *Eat Move and be Healthy*

Abraham H. Maslow, *Toward a Psychology of Being*

Abraham H. Maslow, *The Farther Reaches of Human Nature*

Ginny Whitelaw, *The Zen Leader*

Robert M. Pirsig, *Zen and the Art of Motorcycle Maintenance*

Deepak Malhotra, *I Moved Your Cheese*

Chip Conley, *How Great Companies Get Their Mojo From Maslow*

Eckhart Tolle, *The Power of Now*

Arne Maus, *Forget About Motivation*

Stephen Covey, *The 7 Habits of Highly Effective People*

Deepak Chopra, *The 7 Spiritual Laws of Success*

Paul Herr, *Primal Management*

Dave Logan, John King & Halee Fischer-Wright, *Tribal Leadership*

Viktor E. Frankl, *Man's Search for Meaning*

Viktor E. Frankl, *The Will to Meaning*

Michael Jordan, *I Can't Accept not Trying*

Sue Knight, *NLP at Work*

Bryan Curtis, *Classic Wisdom for the Professional Life*

John Heider, *The Tao of Leadership*

Tad James and Wyatt Woodsmall, *Time Line Therapy and the Basis of Personality*

L. Michael Hall, *Winning the Inner Game*

L. Michael Hall, *The Matrix Model*

Richard Bandler and John Grinder, *Reframing: Neuro Linguistic Programming and the Transformation of Meaning*

Richard Bandler and John Grinder, *Frogs into Princes: Neuro Lingusitic Programming*

WEBSITES

www.carrollconsultancy.com

www.aliciadunams.com

www.identity-compass.com

www.primallifestyle.com

www.alanweiss.com

www.peakorganizations.com

www.tmbusiness.org

www.eckharttolle.com

www.chopracentremeditation.com

www.chopra-online.com

www.williamtrubridge.com

www.verticalblue.net

www.equilibrio.com.au

www.neurosemantics.com

www.nlpcoaching.com

www.tonyrobbins.com

www.amaize.org

www.metacoachfoundation.org

CREDIT TO SOURCES

I WAS INSPIRED to write this by Leo Tolstoy after reading 'A Calendar of Wisdom' as I felt it accurately described my process and intentions when writing this book.

My thoughts collected here come from a large number of works and collections that I have both read in books and attended in trainings over the past 20 years. I have done my best to indicate the source of each point, diagram, or part of the book, although I may not have always marked the exact source, book title, date, or work from which I took it. I translated these thoughts not directly from their original source but from my experience, interpretations, and learnings from these sources. Sometimes my translations may not be identical to the originals. Readers might tell me that my interpretations might not be from the source or completely accurate, but I don't think that there is anything wrong in conveying their thoughts in the context of Evolutionary Leadership for the benefit and good of all.

Readers are welcome to share this information as long as they quote the source as written in this book. If readers would like to translate this book into another language, I would recommend to not look for original quotes but translate directly from my writing. Another reason my thoughts may not correspond exactly to the originals is that I summarized lengthy texts or I have expressed it in my own words. I have done this because the purpose of this book is not to give exact word-for-word translations of thoughts created by other authors or trainers, but to use the great and wonderful heritage created by different contributors, writers, and developers. This is done for the purpose to present to a wide-reading audience an easily accessible everyday circle of reading which will arouse the readers best thoughts and feelings.

MORE PRAISE FOR
THE EVOLUTIONARY LEADER

"I had been waiting on the edge of my seat to read The Evolutionary Leader and I can put my signature on it and say that this will take my coaching to the next level. Thanks Timothy for leading me to the Path and being my guide when I was in need of it!"

Lee Baxter - Head Goalkeeper Coach, Supersport United FC, South African Premier League

"Yet another clear message from Timothy J. Carroll who sets the frame on how you can get amazing results by evolving your leadership. While the changes you do doesn't have to be dramatic, the outputs most likely will be. The Evolutionary Leader gives you loads of inspiration. Having worked with Timothy for my development and in helping other leaders in my organization, I guarantee that what is written is both genuine and possible."

Henrik Holck-Clausen - Vice President of Human Resources at Schneider Electric Norway AS

"What an enlightening book Timothy J. Carroll has given us based on his practical experience as a world class athlete and consultant of leaders in multi-national companies. If you don't read any other book except The Evolutionary Leader this year, you won't be disappointed. Thank you for the tools of change."

Christer Sjostrom - former Senior Vice President, Nordic Baltic Zone - Solutions and Services at Schneider Electric

"Timothy J. Carroll describes, in an easy to read way, how the human mind functions and how leaders make use of it. He reveals how to shift your performance and understanding of how you work as a human being. These steps are simple yet powerful and get dramatic results for the reader."

H. Arne Maus - Main Developer & Senior Consultant, Identity Compass / Author of *Forget about Motivation*

LET'S CONNECT

You can follow Timothy on Twitter at
www.twitter.com/Selfinsight

Connect with Timothy on Facebook or LinkedIn at
www.facebook.com/CarrollConsultancyGroup
www.linkedin.com/in/timothycarroll

View Timothy's official web page at
www.carrollconsultancy.com